The
Wage-Price
Problem

JOHN M. CLARK

Published by
Committee for Economic Growth without Inflation
THE AMERICAN BANKERS ASSOCIATION

The
Wage-Price
Problem

JOHN M. CLARK

THE
AMERICAN
BANKERS
ASSOCIATION

1875

Foreword

THE American Bankers Association considers it a privilege to publish this study by one of America's most distinguished economists of one of the most important economic problems of our time.

John Maurice Clark needs no encomiums from us. Emeritus Professor of Economics at Columbia University, author of many outstanding books and articles, and a past president of the American Economic Association, Dr. Clark long ago attained top rank among American economists.

Some readers may wonder why a monograph such as this is being published by The American Bankers Association. The basic answer is that the wage-price problem has now become a matter of vital concern to all those who wish to achieve sustained economic growth without inflation. Publication of this study reflects the fact that The American Bankers Association is attempting to do its share to contribute to this objective.

In the past the Association has quite naturally concerned itself primarily with the financial aspects of public economic policy. Until recent years, most bankers, along with many others, hoped that if we could adhere to sensible monetary and fiscal policies, the other problems involved in achieving satisfactory growth and reasonably stable prices, would be minimized.

The events of recent years have made it clear, however, that sound financial policies, while still essential, will not suffice alone. We can no longer blink the fact that the combined effects of industrial wage and pricing policies have now come to constitute a persistent inflationary force in our economy.

In 1959 The American Bankers Association launched an enlarged, long-range program to promote economic growth and to combat inflation. In doing so, it was explicitly recognized that attention should be given to certain strategic problems outside the field of banking and finance, and notably to the wage-cost-price spiral.

iii

This is a problem to which the Association had given little study and with which most bankers have had little firsthand experience. We therefore surveyed the research and literature on this subject to see whether we could find materials which would provide a good basis for our educational activities and policy positions.

This search was unsuccessful. While much work has been done in this area, most of it is fragmentary, inconclusive or biased. The objective, balanced synthesis which we sought apparently did not exist.

We therefore decided to see whether such a document could be produced. Our best hope seemed to lie in enlisting the services of an eminent scholar, an economist widely known for his objectivity, his careful research, his analytical skill, and his ability to organize and synthesize complex subject matter.

John Maurice Clark was an obvious choice. Fortunately, he regarded our commission as an intriguing challenge, and made room for it in his working agenda. The ultimate result was this monograph on "The Wage-Price Problem."

Needless to say, the views expressed by Professor Clark are not necessarily those of The American Bankers Association. Indeed, many bankers would doubtless take exception to various points, just as would many businessmen, union officials and academicians.

It seems clear, however, that if we are to work out reasonable solutions to the difficult problems confronting the United States today, we need the insights which our best thinkers can provide.

CASIMIR A. SIENKIEWICZ, *Chairman*
Committee for Economic Growth
without Inflation
The American Bankers Association

May, 1960

Contents

vi

Chapter I. The Problem

1. HAVE WE A NEW AND SECULAR INFLATIONARY TENDENCY?

THERE is a widespread belief that since 1953 the American economy has experienced a new kind of inflation, different from the customary kind which is frequently called "classical"; the new kind being "built into" the present nature of our economy, presaging a continuing inflationary trend in peacetime and in the absence of the "classical" causes.

For our purposes, inflation will mean simply a widespread rise in prices, raising the average level. To this Gardiner C. Means and some others would add that it extends into both flexible and non-flexible types of prices.

Still simplifying, the "classical" type is one in which prices are conceived as *pulled* up by an excess of total monetary demand over the limitations that are set on the supply side. These limitations may come from a literally limited supply or from limits on increase of output set by limited productive capacity or costs that increase as output increases, or by both acting jointly. The excess demand need not be universal, if resources from areas of unused capacity cannot be mobilized to meet the pressures in shortage areas.

The "new" type is one in which prices are apparently *pushed* up by direct action of sellers, without any prior excess demand. The expanded dollar requirements of business at the increased price levels are generally met out of the elastic resources of our flexible credit system, this monetary expansion being an induced enabling factor, not an initiating cause.

TYPES OF "PUSHED-UP" INFLATION

While this describes the clearest and most unmixed case of "pushed-up" inflation, one should recognize that the bearings of price and wage policies on inflation include cases of a more mixed sort. In one mixed type, localized increases in the price-wage structure—localized geographically or by industries—which were induced by local excesses of demand, may spread to other sectors, in which the excess of demand is not directly felt. In a second mixed type, prices or wages may have a one-sided response to fluctuations of demand— being flexible upward more readily than downward—with the result that their response to a series of fluctuations exhibits a "rachet-action," resulting in an upward trend over a long-term period.[1]

These two "mixed" cases have in common the same element that marks the unmixed case: namely, the capacity of wages or prices to rise, independently of excess demand in the particular market where the rise takes place; or to resist a decline in the face of reduced demand. The same factors that can produce the unmixed case can more easily produce these mixed cases. One is taking the bull by the horns if one focuses on the unmixed case.

This "pushed-up" type of inflation has come into attention in the period following the mild Korean War inflation of 1950-1951, since which time general excess demand has been absent. Especially in the recession of 1957-8, prices rose despite a shrinkage of aggregate demand, thus affording a clear case in which prices must have been pushed up by some combination of administered prices and negotiated wages.

Having thus come into attention, the origins of "pushed-up" inflation have been traced, as one element in mixed situations, back to World War II.[2] The present writer, when an OPA consultant, thought he perceived forces of the "push-up" type in 1941, and distinguished the two types at that time.[3] More broadly, failures of prices to follow the

[1] Cf. Thomas A. Wilson, U.S. Congress, Joint Economic Committee, *An Analysis of the Inflation in Machinery Prices*, Study Paper No. 3, esp. p. 61, Nov. 5, 1959.

[2] Cf. J. P. Lewis, "The Problem of Price Stabilization," *American Economic Review*, May, 1959, pp. 309, 312.

[3] See *How to Check Inflation*, Public Affairs Pamphlet No. 64, p. 3.

course indicated by the classical model have been traced much farther back by H. G. Moulton.[1]

CLASSICAL INFLATION

Classical inflation occurs during wars, during peace-time periods of large and persistent public deficits, and during cyclical upswings of business. In the latter case, however, a distinction may be made between booms and the initial stages of recovery from depressed periods when prices and profits are abnormally low, the latter being often called "reflation."

This distinction is naturally difficult to identify by a sharp boundary-line, hinging as it does on a conception of a "normal" midpoint which appears, under business-cycle analysis, to lack the characteristics of a potentially stable equilibrium.

We need not be concerned with fluctuations if prices move in both directions with equal freedom. The prices that are strategic for the "new" inflation are relatively insensitive to cyclical movements—some say at the expense of accentuating fluctuations in physical production and employment—but over the longer trend they appear to contain an inflationary bias of their own.

This takes the three forms already mentioned, including the "rachet-action" that results where prices oppose downward pressures (unless extreme) with a resistance that comes close to a veto, whereas their response to upward pressures is merely slowed-down and restrained. The direct upward drive appears most clearly where strong unions are dealing with employers who have enough market power to charge a wage increase to the customer. This seems to be a prevalent pattern in the *mores* of price-setting and collective bargaining which have grown up in the last two decades.

The pattern acts in combination with the interplay between industries and trades in which productivity increases at different rates, causing differences in their ability to pay

---

[1] See *Can Inflation Be Controlled?* (Washington: 1958), *passim* and esp. Appendices A & B.

increased wages without raising prices.

The present writer is convinced that this upward bias exists and is an important factor, not yet adequately analyzed and demanding serious attention. This appears to accord with the prevailing balance of informed opinion.

CURRENT DIFFERENCES OF OPINION

Within this view, opinions differ as to how serious the prospect is, and as to the relative responsibility of "administered prices" and negotiated wages, also as to the relative importance of this group of factors and those centering in aggregate supply and demand, which are emphasized in the more conventional theories.

Room is afforded for differences of emphasis because wages, for example, are both costs of production, entering as such into the "push-up" type of theory, and also incomes, constituting a source of demand for products. All but the most extreme advocates of the classical theory admit the importance of both kinds of forces.

This most extreme opposition to the "cost-push" theory is represented by the "Chicago group," which adheres to the quantity theory of money as a key to interpretation, by which aggregate demand is presented as the money supply multiplied by its velocity of circulation, and this is equal to the physical volume of trade, multiplied by the price level. In equation form, $MV = PT$. This is a tautology, proving nothing by itself. It acquires causal meaning on the assumption that M, V and T are determined independently of P, and P is determined as a resultant.

Probably no group holds that this is rigidly true or causally all-sufficient; but the group in question tends to argue that there is no convincing evidence that price-level behavior has been different from what would probably have happened in the absence of labor unions and administered prices.[1] This

---

[1] See testimony of Milton Friedman and R. T. Selden, U. S. Congress, Joint Economic Committee, *Employment, Growth, and Price Levels*, Hearings, Part 4 (Washington: 1959), pp. 605-719, esp. pp. 649-668, 688-719. By way of critical analysis of the arguments there presented, two or three sample points may suffice. Causal priority may be inferred from priority of movements in time (though

is used to refute the idea that changes affecting price levels can be generated within the structure of costs and prices themselves.

After serious examination of the arguments and evidence, the present writer remains convinced that such changes are both real and important, among the factors that determine price levels. If prices can move independently, this means that the other terms of the equation adjust (or adjustment may be mutual). If prices are pushed up, money (including credit equivalents) may expand, as it has capacity to do, and velocity may increase; and under current conditions these enabling reactions appear sufficient to handle fairly sizeable movements, automatically or through deliberate policy. If these enabling reactions were insufficient, physical volume of production might be restricted.

ARGUMENTS THAT PUSHED-UP INFLATION EXISTS

Perhaps the strongest argument for the existence of pushed-up inflation is that of H. G. Moulton.[1] He tends to hold that in the case of most prices, demand does not pull them up directly; they are set by sellers, with a view to demand but also under the necessity of covering costs. Costs

---

[1] See *Can Inflation Be Controlled?* (Washington: 1958).

---

this is not fully conclusive). Friedman correlates peaks of general business with peaks in the *rate of change* of the money stock, finds that the latter shows a lead, and infers causal priority. *(Op. cit.,* pp. 616, 638-9). This correlation is fallacious because changes in the rate of change of any cyclical quantity, such as money stocks, precede changes in the total quantity itself, by what would be a full quarter-cycle if the cyclical movements of both were perfectly regular. Therefore Friedman's chart is entirely consistent with the conclusion that peaks and troughs of money stock lag behind peaks and troughs of business volume; and the preceding chart, correlating money stock with money income, corroborates this for the relevant period — say from 1943 on. Movement of money stock lags behind movement of income, and income velocity takes up the slack. Selden *(op. cit.,* pp. 706-718) attempts to dismiss this adaptive behavior of velocity by saying in effect that no reason for it can be found in any of the determinants of velocity *which his theory recognizes,* ignoring the hypothesis that he is supposedly testing: namely, that velocity can respond directly to the needs of business volume. It did so during this period, as his own figures show. On pages 712-13 he cites six industries as cases refuting the cost-push theory, five of which appear to the present writer to exhibit pushed-up inflation accompanied by a cost increase. In general this line of argument shows a tendency to infer that if *any* element of increased demand can be found, even in part of a situation, this discredits the idea that forces may also act from the price-cost side. The more prevalent view leaves room for both kinds of action.

are the "propelling" or "motivating" force, and wage costs are dominant.[1] Others deny that wages are responsible and assign sole responsibility to administered prices and to the profit margins which they protect.[2] We shall argue that both are jointly responsible, in that neither one acts in the way that price stability demonstrably requires.

Argument for the existence of pushed-up inflation faces the usual difficulties of isolating causes in a much-mixed situation. The first bits of evidence come from observed behavior, when strong unions get wage increases, in excess of increases in productivity, from employers who are able to charge the resulting increased cost to the customer, even when there is no excess demand. Second is the further observed fact that, instead of forcing other wages and prices down by absorbing an increased share of a limited total of monetary demand, these increases spread and become general. Third is the fact that the observed overall movements exhibit the effects of such actions. Fourth and most convincing is the analysis of the forces and processes that bring all this about: that explain why the parties act in ways that raise wage-costs and prices. This cannot be summarized in a sentence; it will occupy much of the discussion that follows.

As against such considerations, the contrary view—that these exercises of market power do not affect the outcome, appears to rest on more unsubstantial conjecture. This is especially true of the inherently-unverifiable conjecture that the outcome does not differ substantially from that which would be brought about in any case by the overruling forces of supply and monetary demand. As to policy implications, this latter view appears to prejudge the delicate and debatable question of the power and function of the credit system in controlling the course of prices, tending to assign it a role greater than it may be able to fulfil.

To sum up, the present writer's judgment is that inflationary pressures of the "pushed-up" variety can and do exist.

[1] *Op. cit.*, p. 159.

[2] For a strong presentation of this case, with reference to the steel strike, see Gardiner C. Means, *Administrative Inflation and Public Policy*, (Washington: 1959).

2. IF THE "NEW" INFLATION EXISTS, HOW SERIOUS IS THE PROSPECT?

COMPARED to the violent dimensions which classical inflations frequently or typically assume, the new inflation appears so moderate that it may need some explaining why people are as exercised about it as they appear to be.

In this country, World War II and its traceable aftermath have more than doubled the prewar price level and halved the real value of the prewar dollar, while the new inflation, over the past six or seven years, has not amounted to much more than two per cent per year. Why get excited about that? The main answer is twofold.

First, classical inflations spring from causes that are expected to be temporary, whereas the new inflation offers a probability of a secular tendency extending indefinitely into the future. Indeed, much of the acuteness of current reactions may be a compound effect of disappointed expectations that inflation would end with the end of formal hostilities—we thought it was over, and are doubly disturbed to find that it isn't. It is one thing for groups that have suffered from wartime inflation to write off their losses and face the uncomfortable prospect of adjusting to a fifty-cent dollar. It is far more disturbing to face a dollar in process of further continuous shrinkage. Such a prospect, even if not regarded as a certainty, comes to be built into our structure of expectations, breeding attempts to hedge against it, with results that may both stimulate the movement and distort the structure of investments.

Cost-of-living escalators in wage contracts have multiplied; and the prices of common stocks have been bid up to levels on which their yields are far below those of good bonds, on which interest rates are abnormally high.[1] As to this, Winfield W. Riefler has made the point that, whether the original impulse comes from cost or demand, such expectations add a superstructure of demand-inflation, including

---

[1] High prices of stocks also represent in part the prospect of sharing in physical growth, financed by the plowing-back of earnings.

abnormal stimuli to borrow, even at high interest rates, and invest in equities and speculative assets. How far all this will go, and in what directions it may turn, cannot be confidently predicted; but it clearly contains features that do not make for maximum health in the economy.

Second, the remedy for classical inflation is known: namely, restrictions on spending such as may be brought about by a tight fiscal policy and a restrictive credit policy. Such remedies are clearly necessary if and when excess demand appears; and credit authorities must have freedom to exercise judgment on the delicate and involved question whether such conditions exist, including "realistic" standards of adequate employment. But credit restriction does not reach the causes of pushed-up inflation, is insufficient to prevent it, and if used stringently in a determined attempt to control the level of prices in the absence of excess demand, there is a real possibility that it might make things worse by restricting production and employment to levels which all would agree were undesirably low, without assurance of stopping a creeping price inflation.

Yet there is pressure toward such questionable use of credit restriction, because other suggested remedies are either unacceptable or do not promise to be effective. We are left groping for remedies under which stable levels of prices can be combined with vigorous growth under an economic system that preserves the essentials of freedom and voluntary agreement.

3. POSSIBLE OUTCOMES

THERE is always the possibility that this apparently built-in trend may taper off and come to an end. This prospect depends on a more rapid rate of increase in productivity per man-hour, coupled with a slowing of the prevailing rate of wage-increases, so as to bring the two quantities substantially together.[1] Neither of these changes can be counted on

---

[1] For a persuasive statement, see E. L. Dale, Jr., ''Forecast: No More Inflation?'' *New York Times Magazine*, August 2, 1959, pp. 8ff. In a more moderate

to materialize. A backhanded support for this possibility may be derived from the consideration that the current state of practice and expectations was built up during the war and postwar period — say, 1940-48 — when conditions invited large wage demands; and that normal peace-time conditions may promote a gradual acceptance of more modest expectations. This cannot be dependably counted on, and at best will be gradual. The 1959 steel crisis publicized lip-service to the idea of a non-inflationary wage adjustment; but this means different things to the two sides, and in neither case does it fulfil all the requirements of a really non-inflationary adjustment for the economy as a whole—as will be demonstrated in a later chapter. A secular inflationary trend remains a probability.

MEANING OF PRICE LEVEL STABILITY

But first, what is a stable or non-inflationary price level? The question is worth asking, if only because practically none of the many experts who discuss the subject make any attempt to define it, with the result that the highly-important line between "stability" and "creeping inflation" is left fatally vague. In common sense, stability does not preclude fluctuations of one or all of the principal price indexes, and does not require that ups and downs must exactly offset one another. What it does require is that the ups should not exceed the downs persistently enough to show a readily identifiable trend, making a further rise seem sufficiently probable to cause people to act on that probability. This last is the real test, and it does not preclude some long-term upward drift, if it is slight enough to be disguised in the fluctuations. A trend of as much as 1% per year would be hard to disguise, especially as people are learning to discount dips in the flexible prices, such as foods, and look elsewhere for signs of the trend. In contrast, "creeping inflation" is best identified as a trend persistent enough to create

tone, John T. Dunlop makes a similar suggestion, in U.S. Congress, Joint Economic Committee, *Employment, Growth, and Price Levels*, Hearings, Part 8 (Washington: 1959), p. 2747. Cf. also Committtee for Economic Development, *Defense Against Inflation* (New York: May 1958).

expectations of its continuance, on which people will act. And it is a crucial fact that business men and investors may act on a probability while statistical experts maintain their sophisticated brand of uncertainty about future prospects— as some of them do today. Beginning at this none-too-exact borderline, one may distinguish ''creeping inflation,'' up to perhaps 2% or possibly 2½% per year, accelerated creeping inflation, up to perhaps twice that rate, and runaway or galloping inflation. These have different consequences; and for our purposes the question is whether creeping inflation has inherent tendencies to turn into the more rapid varieties.

WHY INFLATION TENDS TO SPEED UP

For the inherent tendency of creeping inflation to speed up, three main causes appear. One is illustrated by the hypothetical example of a 4% increase in money wages, half of which is cancelled by rising prices, with the result that the next demand is for a 6% increase in an attempt—necessarily self-defeating—to make the 4% increase real as well as adding further increases. And so on, in an increasing spiral.[1] Admitting that this tendency exists, it appears probable that: (1) it is already embodied in typical wage demands, and: (2) it could not be carried very much farther without reaching the kinds of limits that wage-bargainers appear to recognize and respect. On this basis, some increase in the rate of wage-increases is possible, but an indefinite progressive speeding-up appears highly improbable. The prospect is disturbing enough without this added element.

Second: an essentially similar effect might be produced by the universal use of cost-of-living escalator clauses in wage contracts. There is an obvious presumption that these clauses make wages rise faster than they otherwise would, but the presumption is not conclusive, because we do not know what the alternative would be: that is, what kinds of wage stipulations would be exacted in the absence of these

---

[1] See CED, *Defense Against Inflation*, pp. 40-41. For a more general discounting of the danger of a runaway outcome, see John P. Lewis, ''The Problem of Price Stabilization,'' *Amer. Econ. Rev.*, May, 1959, pp. 309, 314-315.

escalator clauses. Does labor get more, or less, in the way of inflationary wage increases in this form than they would have gotten in the form of direct wage increases if escalator clauses had not been available? They may be cheaper than alternative forms of protection, especially as they do not add their inflationary bit unless inflation has materialized. If, by adding a cost-of-living escalator clause, workers could be induced to accept genuinely non-inflationary wage-rates, this would be cheaper than a higher wage rate without the escalator clause, because in the former case inflation would not materialize and the escalator clause would not come into effect. The trouble comes when escalators are superimposed on inflationary wage rates; in which case they may add to the total cost and total inflationary effect.

Third comes the effect of hedging transactions in the markets. Here one must distinguish the purchase of existing equity assets, such as land and common stocks, from things like additional accumulation of inventories or construction of productive facilities ahead of demand. The latter adds to the demand for current products, while the former does not, except as investors or speculators may spend some of the capital gains which inflationary markets bring them. And the expectation that creates the incentive to buy for hedging purposes is also an incentive to reinvest such capital gains, rather than treat them as spendable income. The hedging investor expects to lose in terms of real value if he does no better than maintain the dollar value of his holdings unchanged. Thus, while some spending of capital gains is natural, it appears likely to play a much smaller role in a hedging boom than in a boom not connected with expectations of an inflationary trend.

As for forward capital construction or enlarged accumulation of inventories, there are prudential reasons against heavy forward investment which continue to have weight. In each case, including consumers' durables, advance buying or construction involves committing oneself to something that may turn out inferior to what one might have had if one had waited. When an industry replaces its most obsolete equipment, it will not want to replace it with equipment that may in turn be semi-obsolescent before it is needed. This kind of consideration appears likely to outweigh the small prospective gains from investing at a price that forestalls a year's or a half-year's instalment of a really creeping inflation.

DANGER OF INFLATION ACCELERATING

To sum up, no one of these factors appears likely to have a large effect. Taken all together, it is conceivable that they might cause a creeping inflation to move up into the accelerated class. If that should happen, and should become evident, it would probably arouse effective opposition, even among those who at present think that a little inflation is a good thing for the economy. The present writer would not expect a creeping inflation to accelerate itself, by such internally-generated forces as we have been discussing, beyond, let us say, $2\frac{1}{2}\%$ per year. That rate, as a sustained average, would be quite serious enough, and materially higher rates would spell economic calamity. They could hardly be maintained unless hedging transactions had built a superstructure of demand-supported inflation on top of the original creeping movement. In this case, credit restriction would be the appropriate way to deal with the superstructure, and should be able to check it; the problem being to check unproductive speculation without also limiting sound production and employment. But if the original creeping inflation were of the pushed-up variety, credit restriction alone could not and should not be expected to eliminate it.

One practical conclusion is that we need to steer a balanced course between such undue fear of inflation as might accelerate it, and a delusively optimistic confidence that, if we only make up our minds that even slow creeping inflation is an evil, someone will find means by which it can be stamped out. The harsh fact is that no one knows ways that are both acceptable and warranted to achieve such an uncompromisingly-absolute objective. We must explore and experiment, hoping to work out better methods than we now possess.

Is there a danger that creeping inflation may speed up to

the point of runaway or "galloping" inflation as a result of people's anticipations and their attempts to protect their interests? This calls for a reinforcing factor much more powerful than the hedging methods that are nowadays in evidence, brought about by the prospect of a creeping trend. It appears to involve something more than a moderate increase in the velocity of money, such as the last twelve years have witnessed, the impact of which is potentially controllable. Galloping inflation requires a degree of distrust of the dollar that produces a "flight from cash" to commodities. To bring this about, it seems that the risks of holding cash while it loses buying power must exceed the risks of holding particular commodities or available assortments of commodities, with all the uncertainties to which particular commodities are subject.

The kind of creeping inflation we have so far experienced has not come within hailing distance of this point. The first symptoms would presumably appear in an abnormal expansion of business inventories, such as shows no signs of occurring at present. A subsequent symptom — especially if credit were restricted — could be a pathological increase in monetary velocity. As for the full result, it requires uncontrollable public deficits or other conditions of violent classical inflation. It is inconceivable that it should arise from an upward cost-price push in the absence of excess demand.

DANGER OF SUBSEQUENT DEFLATION

There is the further apprehension that inflation may lead to a corresponding deflation, in which prices, wages, production and employment would all be involved in a general depression. To find grounds for this apprehension, one must not rely on a mere general belief that "what goes up must come down," which has been belied in recent instances, but must look at the kind of inflation we are now experiencing, and ask what features of it might expose it to a drastic reversal, and what events might bring the reversal about. If, despite the considerations just presented, a runaway inflation should develop, it would present a fresh problem, to be dealt with as it arises. In our present and prospective price structure, the most vulnerable sector consists of the prices of common stocks and other equity assets, from which a revulsion might squeeze out the large elements of value that represent a capitalization of expected price inflation. There would remain, however, the capitalization of the equity interest in continued expansion of physical production, unless there should be a departure from the present custom of expanding productive facilities out of reinvested earnings, in favor of the issuance of new securities. Such a squeezing-out of values might conceivably be precipitated by a cyclical recession severe enough to reverse the current state of expectations.

On the whole, this does not appear likely unless we choose to bring it about by using overly-severe general fiscal and credit restrictions in the attempt to combat price inflation, in the face of the likelihood that they would restrict production and employment more than prices, and without eliminating the sources of the kind of price inflation we now face. It seems highly improbable that we should make such excessive use of fiscal and credit restrictions or that we should persist in it after its depressive effects become evident.

4. THE IMPACT OF SECULAR INFLATION

ONE basic fact is that the effects of inflation depend both on its extent and on its character. They involve three kinds of effects: the direct and identifiable effects on recipients of different kinds of income, who may gain or lose in real purchasing power; the much more conjectural effects on the general growth and productiveness of the economy; and effects in modifying and possibly distorting the relative adjustments of prices in the system and the resulting incentives to different kinds of investment and production.

If creeping inflation should turn runaway, the impact would be disastrous on the first count and strongly unfavorable on the other two. It would be ruinous to classes with fixed incomes, or incomes that fail to keep pace with the shrinkage of the dollar, in favor of successful speculators and those who succeed in keeping their money incomes ahead in the race against depreciation. And it would disturb the basis for rational business planning. While many enterprises would profit, some hugely and undeservedly, many would find that their nominal profits had turned into losses, some of which might be ruinous, as the real value of capital assets virtually disappeared while their nominal value was maintained. All this does not need proving.

EFFECTS OF CREEPING INFLATION

But if creeping inflation does not turn runaway, or if it can be prevented from doing so, we are dealing with a lesser order of distortion of incomes, while on the score of effects on growth and productiveness, one wing of opinion holds that the effects are on balance favorable. The most serious distributional effect is on people dependent on fixed money incomes, while people only partly dependent on such incomes suffer in proportionately less degree. These include annuitants, holders of insurance policies and other savers whose funds and financial *savoir faire* do not suffice for hedging against inflation by holding diversified common stocks. It is often said that debtors gain at the expense of creditors, and this is true on the average, though whether a particular debtor gains or not depends on whether the income out of which he must meet his liabilities has expanded or remained constant in money terms. The losers include endowed institutions, such as schools, colleges and hospitals, to the extent that their endowments yield fixed incomes; and this difficulty is reflected in the salaries they can pay their employees and may be concentrated in inadequate increases in teachers' salaries as against the wages of unionized employees of departments of buildings and grounds, or construction workers on the new buildings made necessary by increasing numbers of students.[1]

---

[1] Cf. CED, *Defense Against Inflation*, p. 11; also G. L. Bach, *Inflation*, pp. 3, 23-26.

Here we are getting into the category of workers whose pay, while increasing in money terms, has failed to keep up with the rise in the cost of living, so that in real terms it has shrunk. Then there are others whose real compensation has risen, but by less than the economy-wide average increase in productivity, which is what they would have gotten if the gains from increased productivity had been distributed equally.

An oversimplified example of the impact of inflation at a rate of 2% a year, continued and compounded, might be a worker who at the age of thirty is saving for a retirement annuity. The dollars he saves at thirty will have lost half their purchasing power when he retires at sixty-five. Dollars he saves at twenty will have lost 59% of their value, while dollars he saves at forty and fifty will have retained the majority of their value and may carry greater weight, since his pay will presumably have increased with seniority, and his annuity contributions or other savings may have increased correspondingly. The interest on his savings, if added to them, will more than cancel the creeping depreciation of his principal, so that from this standpoint alone he might be rated as having lost only in the sense of getting less than half the nominal return on his lifetime investment. But this may mean that the retirement income planned or contracted for has shrunk in buying power until it will not support even a modest scale of living.

IS GRADUAL INFLATION A STIMULANT?

It is argued that a gradually-rising price level is a stimulative condition for the economy, favorable to a rapid increase in real incomes. A leading exponent of this general view was the late Sumner H. Slichter. Others have vigorously denied this, pointing out that we have had rapid economic gains in times of stable, rising or falling price levels. Either conclusion may be too simple; in terms of effects, it is inherently probable that a demand-induced inflation is more favorable to expansion than one pushed up from the cost-price side, and that a spontaneous price-reduction is more favorable than one enforced by restrictive measures. A spontaneously stable price level may be more favorable to growth than creeping inflation. But it is also likely that mild inflation is a more stimulative condition than one marked by such drastic restrictions as would be necessary to stamp it out. It appears that wisdom lies in limiting restrictions short of this point and seeking further for remedies for the remaining residuum of inflation, and that in this sense the hardships resulting from this residuum are lesser evils, pending our finding of better answers than we now have.

As to these hardships, the claim that a gradually rising price level stimulates the increase of real incomes has been made the basis for the further claim that this makes it possible to take care of most cases of hardship by increasing social security allowances enough to outweigh the shrinking of the dollar and leave the recipients better off in real terms than people in corresponding situations were before the increase in prices.[1] The increase in social security allowances is a fact, and is facilitated by the increase of our national income; but there is no proof, and can be none, that the price inflation made the country's economic expansion greater than it would have been with a stable price level. The improved provision is also due to changes in social outlook and to political pressures that would have caused increasingly liberal allowances without the special incentive of the need to offset the shrinkage of the social security dollar. How much each factor contributed can only be conjectured.

These factors could affect social security pensions, and could cause increases in the liberality of other pensions, but would not affect annuities actuarially calculated on the basis of the annuitant's own contributions, or these plus fixed contributions by his employer. Nor would they affect personal

---

[1] One limited and tentative expression of this view was given by Robert Eisner, U.S. Congress, Joint Economic Committee, *Employment, Growth, and Price Levels*, Hearings, Part 4, (Washington: 1959), p. 789: "... I might raise the question as to what these pensions might be or have been if over the past 25 years the Government had not followed an expansionary policy.... The price increases have not prevented probably 95 percent of us from being much better off than ... the people who were comparable to us in the social scale were 25 years ago."

savings accumulated prior to inflation by persons whose limited incomes would not permit them the resource of diversified common stocks as investments. Not all of these qualify for social security. As to the great class of white-collar salaried workers, their loss is mainly relative, accentuated by time-lag, though the time-lag may be a serious matter in the case of teachers, and other less publicized types of workers. To sum up, the hardships are subject to many mitigations, but they still fall heavily on large numbers.

EFFECTS ON PROFITS

Two pertinent questions remain. First, if a moderate inflationary trend is a stimulus to an expansion of production, is not this because of profits resulting from *not* having to compensate fully everyone who is unfavorably affected; and if such compensation becomes complete, will the stimulus from rising prices be cancelled? Perhaps not entirely, since the resulting business gains are likely to be more immediate, visible and traceable than eventuating burdens. It seems that any answer is bound to be quite conjectural. If there is doubt whether a creeping rate of pushed-up inflation is favorable or unfavorable to increased production, there appears to be no doubt that more rapid inflation is unfavorable.

Even creeping inflation distorts depreciation accounting, forcing firms to use what are nominally profits to replace their physical capital, and creating a bookkeeping anomaly for which no easy resolution is discernible that would combine strict logic with desirable pragmatic effects. It has been urged that orthodox depreciation on an historical-cost basis provides sufficient funds for actual replacements; but if this is true, it still does not dispose of the accounting function of depreciation in correctly reporting the value of remaining partly-depreciated assets. The chief bearing of all this on our problem is that it forces business firms to report as income amounts that are partly fictitious, being really depreciation. And anything reported as income may be a basis for wage demands.

Perhaps the most substantial retarding effect of inflation on a country's real income arises from its effect on international trade. Inflation in a single country handicaps its exports, stimulates imports that compete with its domestic products, and makes for an unfavorable balance of trade and exchange. If this effect has been partially inhibited by protective trade barriers, it may be brought to light by a lessening of these barriers (we are committed to promoting such a lessening of barriers). Or if the effect has been offset by inflation and economic difficulties in other countries, it may become active as the other countries improve their productivity and their monetary stability (as European countries have been doing recently). This country's balance, already loaded with large foreign aid payments, has turned heavily unfavorable, occasioning great drains on its gold reserve. Though this still includes nearly half the world's gold supply, it is subject to claims from foreign dollar credits as well as to reserve requirements for our domestic money supply. Drains upon it are occasioning some concern, and need to be considered in any decisions on policy affecting our domestic price-level.

5. WHAT IS A DESIRABLE PRICE-LEVEL OBJECTIVE?

As to an acceptable objective for the trend of general prices, the range of prevalent opinion appears to run from regarding any identifiable upward trend as a serious matter, to being willing to accept, or even welcome, an average upward trend as high as 2% per year, meaning, of course, that in some years it would be more. Toward the rationale underlying these judgments, one of the most illuminating approaches is to start with the overall increase in productivity and ask how the resulting gains in real income would be divided under a declining, stationary or rising price level.

IS A DECLINING PRICE LEVEL DESIRABLE?

First comes the old-fashioned idea, to which little attention seems to be paid currently, of the desirability of a price level that declines slowly with increasing productivity and diffuses the resulting gains largely among the whole population in their capacity as consumers. The outstanding exposition of this view is found in the writings of Edwin G. Nourse on price trends.[1] Nourse's present concern is, naturally, with checking serious inflation.[2] The earlier view has what may be a purely accidental kinship with the simplified way in which economic theorists formulated the "law of competitive price" as tending to reduce particular prices to costs, taking factor-prices for granted and leaving overall price levels as a separate problem. It represents the simplest way of diffusing these gains, and the way that benefits all groups alike.

To diffuse them to factors of production, instead of to consumers, is at least equally logical, but more complicated, both in theory and practice, as we shall see in Chapter III. In terms of equity, diffusion through reduced prices has the advantage that persons dependent on fixed money incomes, instead of suffering losses or at best remaining unaffected, would share automatically and fully in the gains of progress. Pragmatically, this would not be favored by those who think that it stimulates progress and expansion if the gains of progress go to the groups actively engaged in production.

The most rigorous form of the theory of price-reduction, implying that factor prices on the average remain unchanged, would mean that unions had lost their most conspicuous and tangible economic function: that of raising the general level of wages,[3] reducing it to a contest in which one

---

[1] See Nourse & Drury, *Industrial Price Policies and Economic Progress*, 1938; and E. G. Nourse, *Price Making in a Democracy*, 1944.

[2] See his "Prices and Policy Makers," *Challenge*, Dec., 1957, pp. 29-44.

[3] This is an indispensable function; but the effect of union action in speeding the rise in real wages, as distinct from money wages, is probably greatly exaggerated — union leaders have an interest in cultivating this exaggeration — and may be judged less important than gains in the imponderable area of human rights on the job.

union's gain is another's loss. Unions have power enough to prevent any such emasculation of their functions. Most students of the problem would probably hold that there is no advantage in a gradually falling price level as against a stationary one, though admitting that a falling level has in the past proved consistent with healthy progress.[1] They would also probably hold that we shall be doing well if, among the producers and industries that show a better-than-average increase in productivity, enough reduce their prices to offset those that must increase their prices on account of a slower-than-average increase in productivity, thus permitting the overall price level to remain stable.

DIVIDING THE GAINS OF PROGRESS

Next in order comes the principle, named by the planning committee formed as part of the Kaiser Steel settlement, that the gains of progress should be divided between workers, employers and the consuming public.[2] This is presumably to be construed as referring to this particular company, and implies some reduction in its prices, such as might be consistent with a stable overall price level, including some increases and some reductions. In this case consumers as such would get no gains, all of which would go to producers; and the active problem would be the division between industries with greater or smaller increases in productivity, and between wages and profits in each industry.

Finally, if the general price level rises, this means that producing groups are absorbing more than the whole increase in productivity, while consumers suffer a loss in their consuming role. For a majority, perhaps, this is made up for by increases in their dollar incomes, but not for all. Such a transfer of real income must, it seems, be regarded as in

---

[1] The post-Civil-War period has been cited. It falls into a rapid deflation down to the resumption of specie payments in 1879, and a slow downtrend from then until 1897. In both subperiods wholesale prices were falling about twice as fast as consumer prices: a discrepancy which may have left an extra margin for profits. It is not proved that a different kind of price decline would show equally good results. This one was hard on farm debtors, and bred Bryan's free silver campaigns.

[2] See *New York Times,* Dec. 9, 1959.

itself undesirable, leaving open the controversial question whether a small amount of it tends to stimulate production. (We have already looked at the fact that more rapid inflations bring more serious consequences.) However, such general judgments of what is desirable or undesirable are of little or no effect unless we know in a more positive way what adjustments between different wages and prices are necessary to a non-inflationary result, why actual adjustments work differently, what instruments we have available to change this behavior and how these instruments are likely to work.

Chapter II. Background Factors Conditioning Price Behavior

1. TYPES OF PRICE BEHAVIOR: FLEXIBLE AND NON-FLEXIBLE PRICES

TYPES of prices and their behavior are obviously central to this problem. This includes price-components, especially wage-costs. Prices may be divided into three broad groups, according as they are (1) set by supply and demand in markets, or are (2) quoted by sellers (or in some cases by buyers), or are (3) negotiated between buyers and sellers or their representatives, the outstanding example for our purpose being wages as fixed by collective bargaining.[1] Or prices may be distinguished according as they are flexible or non-flexible, or according as they are strongly competitive, "administered" but subject to degrees of competitive forces, or strongly monopolistic.[2] This does not cover all the variations and combinations, but may serve as an initial framework for analysis. Each of these distinctions is important for an understanding of the problem of the "new" inflation.

Flexible prices include agricultural products and other basic raw materials, especially those sold on organized exchanges. Secondarily, they include some manufactured products in which flexibly-priced materials are dominant components of costs, as the prices paid for livestock are in the case of packing-house products. Further, to a somewhat less extent, they include various products in which very large numbers of sellers compete actively in the market

---

[1] Market vs. quoted prices are stressed by Moulton, *op. cit.*, esp. pp. 76-84, and the conclusion is drawn that while demand is important, it does not literally "pull" prices up, except for the few that are of the market type.

[2] The basic source for flexible vs. non-flexible prices is Gardiner C. Means, *The Structure of the American Economy*, 1939. For purposes of the present discussion, reference may be made to his pamphlet, *Administrative Inflation and Public Policy*, Anderson Kramer Associates (Washington: 1959). Here he denies that wage-costs played any causal part in the recent inflation, tracing it all to other causes.

[23]

areas in which particular prices are determined. In general, prices of manufactured products are less flexible than those of raw materials, especially where the manufacturing industry is highly concentrated, or where a firm's product is strongly enough differentiated to give the firm considerable latitude within which its pricing policy may depart from those of its closest competitors.

CHARACTERISTICS OF PRICE FLEXIBILITY

Flexibility of prices may be measured by frequency of change or by amplitude, and high frequency and high amplitude tend to go together. Price changes may occur in response to changes in the balance of "demand and supply," or to changes in the balance between price and cost. The most frequent changes are those that occur in response to demand and supply; and if "supply" be interpreted literally, they are confined to the kinds of products of which a supply is first produced and then brought to market to sell for what it will bring. For manufactured products, this kind of pricing is chiefly confined to special sales and disposal of remainders. For most purposes, the producer quotes a price at which he offers to fill orders without any specified limit, and governs his output currently according to the flow of orders received or expected. If sales are unsatisfactory, the producer may try to improve his offering, perhaps changing his price, his marketing policy, his product or a combination of all three. Such adjustments are inevitably less frequent than those of a produce market.

It is this distinction in responses that underlies the generalization that in agriculture the response to a decline in demand is a reduction of price and no reduction of total output — perhaps even an increase — while in large-scale manufacturing the response is a reduction in output, often with no change in price.

For our present purpose the adjustments between earnings and costs are the important ones — far more important than rapid and precise daily adjustment of price to equate demand and supply. For these more important adjustments, ready two-way flexibility is essential, but extreme frequency is not necessary; the frequency commonly found among manufactured products is sufficient for the purpose in hand. And agricultural adjustments *of this sort,* far from being highly flexible, are actually more sluggish and obstructed than those of manufacturing: not sufficiently flexible for the function of protecting earnings that will cover economic costs. This creates a real disadvantage for the flexible-price sector of the economy in dealings with the sectors where pricing is less flexible. The public reaction to this problem — agricultural price supports and attempted restriction of production — is common knowledge. The most notable categories of flexible prices have been made less flexible downward.

ONE-WAY PRICE FLEXIBILITY

One characteristic of really flexible prices is that they are as flexible downward as upward. In contrast, "administered" prices commonly rise less than flexible ones in response to increasing demand, but are less flexible downward than upward, resulting in the "ratchet-action" already mentioned, which tends to leave a net upward residue as a secular trend over a series of fluctuations.[1] This is an enormously important factor in the "new" inflation. The same thing is true of wages as fixed by collective bargaining. They may be generally slower to respond to increased demand than wages in an unorganized market, but their resistance to declines is still greater, amounting to a virtual veto under most conditions; and the resulting ratchet action is powerful.

There is a strong economic presumption against such one-way action and in favor of equal two-way flexibility. From this standpoint it must appear that agricultural price-supports represent the wrong direction in which to narrow the troublesome gap between the price-flexible and price-inflexible sectors of the economy. It may seem self-evident that a system that maintains physical output at the expense of

---

[1] Cf. Gardner Ackley, "Administered Prices Reconsidered," *Amer. Econ. Rev.,* May, 1959, pp. 419-430, esp. p. 425.

price is superior to a system that maintains prices at the expense of physical volume of output and sales.

MAINTAINING DEMAND THROUGH PRICE REDUCTIONS

This raises the question whether the economy would be sounder if manufacturing industries behaved more like one-family farms and responded to a decline in demand by reducing prices until the supply is moved off the market. Perhaps the fairest manufacturing equivalent for the indicated behavior of agricultural prices would be a reduction of price sufficient to restore the initial volume of demand, or perhaps to maintain sales volume at a high and stable ratio to capacity. This implies a readiness to slash prices with no assigned limit in an attempt to move a normal output in the face of subnormal demand. The result could be a cumulative and spreading demoralization that would doom the attempt to failure.

In terms of cost conditions, is it feasible to reduce prices enough to accomplish the end in view? The reductions could not exceed the sellers' profit margins, and these are, on the average, a minor fraction of the total "value added" by manufacture, the greater part being covered by wage costs. So long as the wage costs are rigid downward, feasible price reductions are too limited to have any assurance of being able to restore demand, unless demand is highly elastic; and the same causes that make the demand for many products shrink, also tend to make it inelastic in response to price reductions. The best chance would be if small recoveries of demand, brought about by substantial price reductions, should, by expanding employment slightly, start a spiral of reviving income sufficient to offset the reductions of income resulting from the initial price cuts.

Such a favorable conjunction is highly problematical; it appears more likely that industries reducing their prices would find their earnings threatening to vanish, before the price reductions, by themselves, could bring about revival of demand. This method might work if one key feature of the one-family farm were reproduced: namely, that labor's compensation shared fully in the reductions. And that is out of the question.

2. BUSINESS PRICING: COMPETITIVE, MONOPOLISTIC OR "ADMINISTERED"

INSOFAR as conditions and policies of business pricing have a bearing on inflation, it is naturally the monopolistic or "administered" prices at which attention is first directed. They are open to suspicion of charging more than they need to, thus supporting unnecessarily-liberal "target returns." Strictly speaking, this would not bring about inflation, in the sense of an increase in the price level, unless it were an increasing condition, either because there is a tendency to charge increasing margins of profit, or because liberal profit margins expose firms to progressively-increasing wage demands, which are passed on to customers, perhaps with something added, or because "administered" or monopoloidal prices are coming to cover an increasing proportion of the economy.

PRICING IN COMPETITIVE INDUSTRIES

The standard of comparison is, naturally, drawn from industries and trades in which competitive forces are strong and highly active, and firms cannot fix their profits at discretion, being limited by the need of meeting the rival offers of competing firms. Most such firms try to maximize their profits (or minimize losses) because assurance of survival requires it; the profits are small enough and precarious enough to preclude laxness in this matter. The strongest and lowest-cost firms have a wider latitude for choice of policy. Firms will range downward from these, to those earning substandard returns, and those which at any given time are incurring losses. With respect to the passing-on of increased costs, such industries are not the most shining marks for cost-increasing wage demands; and to the extent that they do have to meet such demands they are under greater necessity to pass them on than less competitive industries are, but may find it a more difficult or painful process. Some marginal firms might be put out of business before prices could be raised to cover the increased costs.

Active competition tends to give prices some flexibility downward, but apparently in a more subdued fashion than often occurred during the last quarter of the nineteenth century, when modern industrial competition was newer, business slumps were more violent and price warfare more frequent. Business mores appear to have developed greater feeling for stability, and avoidance of ruinous excesses of competition.

To sum up, it appears that the highly competitive sectors of the economy are not prime movers in "pushed-up" inflation, but they may, with difficulty, push prices up when costs have risen, and they may have traces of sluggishness in downward price flexibility.

PRICING IN MONOPOLISTIC INDUSTRIES

In contrast, industries that are near the monopoly end of the scale, in terms of their price-behavior, show patterns likely to contribute to this kind of inflation. This group includes near-monopolies and industries so highly concentrated that they follow one another's pricing patterns closely, without formal agreement. They do not set prices to "maximize profit" after the model of the textbooks—not even outright monopolies do that. They are concerned with long-run growth and avoiding encroachments by substitutes or new entries. Within these limits they appear typically to aim at covering a liberal version of "full cost" or a "target return" on volume of sales or on investment.[1] Under current conditions, "full cost" properly includes the costs of physical replacements at prices far above the original costs that are covered by orthodox depreciation charges.

---

[1] See especially Kaplan, Dirlam and Lanzillotti, *Pricing in Big Business*, The Brookings Institution, 1958, also Lanzillotti, "Pricing Objectives in Large Companies," *Amer. Econ. Rev.*, Dec., 1958, pp. 921-940: a summary report of findings of the larger study.

The First National City Bank of New York has compiled profit ratios on sales for forty major industries.

More controversial is the growingly-entrenched practice of providing for expansion out of plowed-back earnings, in addition to cash dividends. When these are added up, they may make a sum of bookkeeping profits that forms a shining mark for wage demands by a strong union. The prices of such firms show pronounced rigidity, they can be raised to shift taxes on net income, at least in substantial part, and quite readily pass on the full amount of increased costs to the customer—more often raising prices in approximately the ratio in which costs have increased. The bearing of all this on the "new" inflation is obvious.

PRICING IN INTERMEDIATE INDUSTRIES

Industries that are concentrated but still substantially competitive show intermediate patterns. Here very strong concerns may, with an eye on the antitrust laws, refrain from pricing low enough to drive out or endanger too many of their smaller competitors. The same consideration might lie behind a general price increase, following an industry-wide wage increase which the strong firms could absorb, but not their weaker competitors. In such industries there is evidence of considerable discretionary policy-making power, and of rates of return earned by strong companies, well above economists' ideas of a normal competitive return.[1] Such returns are an invitation to wage demands from strong unions. Among the competitive forces that exist, competition which is both immediate and direct may be less controlling on the firms' policy than competition or substitution that is indirect or potential and—what is more to the present point—acts too deliberately to be fully effective in combatting some of the tendencies of the "new" inflation.

One familiar view appears to be borne out by the statistics: namely, that highly-concentrated industries pay higher

---

[1] Derived from table, U.S. Congress, Joint Economic Committee, *Employment, Growth, and Price Levels,* Hearings, Part 8, (Washington: 1959), p. 2639. The low-concentration group consisted of lumber, furniture, apparel, leather, cleaning plants, laundries and retail stores; the high-concentration group consisted of petroleum, rubber, chemicals, primary metal (presumably combining ferrous and non-ferrous), machinery, transport equipment and electrical machinery.

wages than industries of the opposite sort, and there is evidence that the differential is increasing. Professor Martin Segal, testifying before the Joint Congressional Committee in 1959, compared groups of seven industries of each sort, finding that the average hourly earnings in 1953 were $1.34 for the "low-wage and low-concentration industries" and $1.97-3/7 for the high-concentration group, while the average increase from 1953-1958 was 16-1/7% for the first group and 23-4/7% for the second.[1] It is to be presumed that profits as well as wages were higher for the concentrated group, and that the more rapid rise in wages was connected with the ability of these employers to charge a wage-rise to the customers. It appears also that wages, even in the low-wage group, rose substantially more than the cost of living. More than this these figures do not show.

3. ACTUAL AND GENERALLY-APPROVED AIMS OF BUSINESS AND LABOR

THE actual aims of business we have just been examining. As for the actual aims of organized labor, the most famous statement of them is Gompers' "more, without limit." This is best construed as a long-run aim for endless progress. For any given wage-negotiation, it is recognized that there are limits on what can be secured, but there is a tendency to think that the employer can safely be left to protect these limits. This assumption is open to question under the prevailing balance of bargaining power, including the employer's ability to pass on cost-increases. Further, this assumption tends toward construing the economic limits in terms of the ability to pay possessed by particular industries or particular employers, and this is not a safe guide for the economy as a whole, because increases secured on this basis tend to spread to industries with less ability to pay them.

---

[1] In The Brookings Institution study, *op. cit.*, of the twenty big companies covered, the range of return on investment for 1947-55 runs from 5.4% for Sears-Roebuck and 6.9% for Swift to 25.9% for duPont and 26% for General Motors. The greatest concentration occurs between 12% and 13%. See Lanzillotti, *op. cit.*, pp. 921, 924-7.

As to generally-approved criteria, there appears to be a somewhat qualified double standard, which might be stated as the highest wages consistent with the necessary share for property and enterprise, and the smallest share for property and enterprise consistent with the returns necessary to enable and to stimulate vigorous improvement and the heavy investment that is needed to implement it. This duality of standard might not make much difference in practice, depending on how liberal this minimum necessary return is judged to be. The point is that, from this prevalent public standpoint, profits are a means to the end of promoting economic growth, efficiency and improvement, while higher wages are regarded as desirable ends in themselves, regardless of the recognized fact that workers take part of the benefit in the form of shorter hours of work, which may or may not be fully made up for by more intelligence and skill on the worker's part. Business men themselves recognize the need of defending profits as reasonable; but they appear to assume without argument the justification for including capital expansion out of earnings in addition to dividends, as part of the necessary return, to protect which price increases are warranted, debatable as this standard is when so employed by firms which have the implied degree of economic power. And employers still attempt to keep their prices as something separate from the issues pertinent to wage-negotiations. How long this attitude can survive the growing interest in "pushed-up" inflation is a question well worth watching.

CRITERIA USED BY ORGANIZED LABOR

Organized labor itself has a number of criteria, from which it selects the ones that will support a wage-increase in the particular case at issue. If the employers appear able to afford an increase, that criterion is uppermost, regardless of whether these workers may be among the highest-paid in the country. If the employers cannot absorb an increase, the ground shifts to emphasis on the workers' disadvantages as compared to others, including those whose employers *could* afford an increase. The fact that the first kind of wage increase leads to the second is an added recommendation: the group in the strongest position sets a pace from which the others benefit. The fact that the sequence necessitates price increases is ignored: price increases are otherwise explained and are grounds for further wage increases. The master criterion appears to be that wage increases in line with customary expectations are always warranted. Apparently, in the steel negotiations of 1959, no other criterion was used.

This all ties in with the exemption of organized labor from the antitrust laws that are applicable to business, and the structure of authorized bargaining-power tactics that has grown up on the basis of this exemption.[1] Competition of low-wage areas is combatted by attempts to organize them and to raise substandard rates. Within the union structure there is potential competition between leaders and possible rivals, or potential rival unions in some cases, but it is a kind of competition that naturally tends to raise wages. It is rivalry in offering prospective gains to the members *via* the use of the union's non-competitive bargaining position in bargaining with the employer. Large wage-gains win the members' support.

The approved criterion for business earnings is based on what healthy competition would presumably bring about, including differentials for superior efficiency and profits or losses for successful or unsuccessful innovation, as tested by rivalry with previous products or processes. Even patents are subject to such rivalry. Underlying this is the view that gains from progress tend soon to become standard practice, available to "representative firms" and no longer a source of differential returns. They are then in the "public domain." Logically, the same principle would apply to wages where successful innovation by employers has led to differential increases in earnings. Criteria for the diffusion of

---

[1] This legally-sanctioned power structure has recently been forcefully analysed by Roscoe Pound; see his *Legal Immunities of Labor Unions*, American Enterprise Association (Washington: 1957).

such wage-differentials have hardly begun to be systematically inquired into.

4. DISPUTE OVER RESPONSIBILITY
FOR INFLATION: AN OBSTACLE
TO CONSTRUCTIVE ACTION

ONE of the chief obstacles to the kind of action that is necessary, if creeping inflation is to be successfully dealt with, is the fact that labor and business each sees the other as the responsible party, and views its own general course of action as basically justified. Each sees the other as the initiating and aggressive party, and itself as responding defensively: labor to offset increases in the cost of living and business to maintain its former rate of profit after a wage increase which raised its wage-costs of production. In the former case, the increased cost of living typically has deprived the workers of only a fraction of the gains from their recent wage-increases, leaving them in the aggregate with as large real gains as are available in the economy. In the case of the employer, it may be argued that he should have absorbed the increased wage-costs, or that he recouped it with a percentage added, thus raising prices by more than costs had been raised. This the employer would defend as maintaining his *pro rata* share. Back of this lies a chronic dispute over how large profits actually are; and back of this lies the problem of a just or economically sound division between wages and profits. Thus the question who is causally responsible for inflation becomes merged with the question of the reasonableness of the distribution of incomes.

The question which moved first and which is trying to catch up, can never be settled, for lack of a clearly neutral base-date to start from. The "new" inflation carries on from thoroughly abnormal wartime conditions in a sequence in which the question of priority is no more meaningful than that of the chicken and the egg. Of course, when prices are raised, it is business that raises them—in this sense it is the initiating factor. But it is always responding to some con-

[33]

dition; and during the period we are concerned with this has almost always been an increase in costs. More meaningful, pragmatically, is the question whether either share is threatened with an encroachment that would place it under a need of catching up. With regard to this, the workers have absorbed the increased cost of living and still gained. If the past ten years' increase in money wages in excess of increased productivity had been absorbed out of profits, profits before taxes would have been reduced catastrophically. Whatever one may think as to whether profits include some that are unnecessarily large, there can be little question that a few years' absorption of increased wage costs at recent rates would encroach on the necessary minimum. Profits would really have to do some catching up.

The main effect of such arguments is to satisfy each party that, whatever needs to be done to cure inflation, it needs to be done by someone else, not by the party in question. To the extent that this attitude prevails, it means that nothing constructive will be done by the parties at issue; the entire burden will be thrown on public agencies. And they are not capable of carrying it on those terms. The following chapter will attempt to show, by a different kind of approach, that if inflation is to be stopped, both parties must alter their customary behavior. In this very practical sense, the responsibility for inflation is shared.

Chapter III. Basic Economic Limits: The Inescapable Arithmetic of Price-Level Stability

1. WHAT A MODEL OF NON-INFLATIONARY BEHAVIOR CAN SHOW

W E have seen that under a stationary price level the gains of increased productive efficiency go to the recipients of the incomes arising from production; and that the remaining problem is how these gains are shared between different industries, and between wages and profits in each industry and firm. In practice, this latter problem comes first, since it is the sharing of the gains, *via* the wages paid and the prices charged in different occupations and industries, that determines what happens to the general price level.

The guiding principle is that of a fully competitive system, in which competition of employers for factors of production ensures that these receive the full value of their contributions to the product, while perfect markets for labor and capital equalize these rewards so that workers of equivalent quality get equal pay. If we had this kind of impossibly-perfect competitive system, there would be no need to try to define the result it would bring about—the system could be left to do that automatically, without any of the participants having any need to understand the end-result to which their separate efforts contribute. If this were the case the occasion for the present memorandum would not exist. But since actual conditions range from severe competition to near-monopoly, it becomes necessary to define the kind of behavior, on the part of the various participants, which is required if a stable price level is to result.

This is the most revealing single thing that can be done toward clarifying the problem of the relation of wage and price policies to inflation. By spelling out the behavior necessary to avoid inflation, it not only sets rational guides for policy, but should serve to resolve the pointless controversy we have just been looking at, between groups each of which lays the whole responsibility on the other.

Most discussion of this problem consists of uncoordinated bits and pieces, precisely because it is not organized around the kind of comprehensive specification of requirements that is here attempted. Almost no one even makes the attempt to spell out the requirements of a correct solution.[1] One hopes that this is mainly because of the newness of the problem in its present form. We have not lived with it long enough to develop the kind of maturity of attitude toward it which can penetrate the smoke-screens or the sincere myopias of conflicting special interests and draw an integral picture of the common interest. This will be attempted first in a series of simplified categorical propositions, after which the picture will be amplified and the complexities of reality introduced.

2. THE ESSENTIAL ARITHMETIC OUTLINED

(1) THE sum total of real incomes is identical with the total of real wealth produced. The same is true of the annual increase of these quantities. Special wartime conditions gave "real income" a special meaning and enabled it temporarily to exceed the amount of real wealth produced, or to seem to do so. This will be examined later. The annual increase can be measured in various ways; its long-term trend has been remarkably steady at something under 2% per worker. This is the limit on the increase of total real income.

(2) An increase in total money income in excess of the increase in total wealth produced necessarily takes the form of higher prices without increasing real incomes.

(3) Particular individuals or groups can secure a larger-than-average increase in their real incomes by securing a larger-than-average increase in their money incomes, but

---

[1] Two very good condensed statements of the essential arithmetic may be noted. One is by Fritz Machlup, Joint Economic Committee, *op. cit.*, Part 9A, pp. 2828-30, 2853. The other is by the AFL-CIO, Joint Economic Committee, *op. cit.*, Part 9B, p. 3101. It is presented as a theory, but any application is renounced, Joint Economic Committee, *op. cit.*, esp. pp. 3102, 3125.

only to the extent that other groups get less than the average increase.

(4) As between wages and the share going to business enterprise (which will be called "profits" for short), the relative shares have shown marked long-term stability, indicating that there is probably rather limited room for either share to increase at the expense of the other.

(5) When the relative shares remain constant, total real wages per worker can increase only at the same percentage rate at which total real product per worker increases.

(6) In recent years, the fractional share going to wages has apparently increased. While measures of this increase differ, it might enable total real wages per worker to increase by more than the rate of increase of total product per worker, the excess being of the order of magnitude of one tenth of one percent, at a rough estimate. With this addition the basic limiting rate would still be less than 2%.

(7) Product per worker increases at different rates in different industries.

(8) Wage-costs per unit of product in any industry rise, remain constant or diminish, according as wage rates rise more than productivity, proportionately with it, or less. The same relation holds between average wage-costs and average wage-rates for the economy as a whole.

(9) If wage rates in each industry increased at the same rate as productivity in that industry, wage-costs would remain unchanged, and prices, if competitively determined, could remain unchanged so far as governed by costs; but the structure of relative wages would be loaded with grossly inequitable differentials, which at some point would become untenable. This describes the first stage of what may be called the industry-by-industry wage-price adjustment.

(10) In a theoretically perfect labor market, wages for similar grades of labor would be equal, and differentials between grades would be adjusted by competitive forces of demand and supply. This may be designated as an equilibrium wage structure.

(11) In the actual labor market, further differentials per-

sist, due to market friction, to inter-industry differences in the force of competition and in the market power of labor and in rates of increase in productivity; but these further differentials are tolerated by the market only within somewhat indefinite limits. These limits define what may be called the tolerated wage structure.

(12) If changes in wages start on an industry-by-industry basis, the least-favored wages will be raised, faster than productivity in the industries affected, in an attempt to reduce the inequitable differentials. They may not catch up: the differentials may widen for some time, but at the tolerated level they will be much less than productivity differentials. The adjustments, being almost entirely upward, will raise wage-costs of products except where productivity has increased fastest, resulting in increased prices where wage costs have been raised.[1] Thus a general increase in prices results from the industry-by-industry adjustment.

(13) An alternative adjustment would take as its point of departure the limiting of wage increases to the economy-wide rate of increase in productivity (plus the unimportant fraction that might be gained at the expense of profits). This would create no new wage-disequilibria, but would generate increased profits where productivity had increased more than wages, and losses or reduced profits where it had increased less. Equilibrium in the structure of prices and profits would then require that prices be raised where wage-costs had increased because productivity had lagged behind the average rate, and be reduced where wage-costs had been reduced because productivity had exceeded the average rate.

---

[1] An example might be the men's clothing industry, in which the Amalgamated Clothing Workers plan to seek, in 1960, their first general wage increase in four years. Having geared its wage demands to the industry's capacity to pay, the union has lost ground in the past seven years. Its present average hourly rate of $2.12, following a 12½ cent increase in 1956, is far below the 20% average increase for manufacturing from 1955-59 (see Table I, p. 40) and apparently below the increase in cost of living, indicating an absolute decline in real base-wage rates. (See A. H. Raskin, *New York Times*, Dec. 21, 1959, pp. 1, 17. The figures are based on statement by Jacob S. Potofsky, the head of the union.) The conditions indicated by Mr. Potofsky in support of the proposed demand include a labor shortage at current rates, strong demand for the product and an increase in productivity which is, however, insufficient to obviate a need for increased prices.

(14) A more realistic adjustment, still consistent with a stable price level, would occur if wage differentials occurred to the extent permitted by the "tolerated" wage structure, so long as the average wage increase did not exceed the average increase in productivity, and prices were lowered where wage-costs per unit had been reduced, and raised only where wage-costs had been increased.[1]

(15) This adjustment could hardly be expected to be perfectly carried out; but under favorable conditions it might be approximated closely enough to leave the expected movement of prices uncertain, thus avoiding the consequences of inflationary expectations, already discussed.

(16) Such an outcome requires (a) restraint in organized labor's use of its market power, either voluntary or enforced by employers' stiff resistance, and (b) ready downward flexibility of prices where the state of costs and profits permits. These requirements are linked together, since if profits above a competitive minimum are not passed on promptly to customers, they offer a target for wage demands which unions will not ignore.

(17) In the present American economy, neither of these essential conditions for the avoidance of inflation exists: the balance of bargaining power is tilted in an inflationary direction. This is because, while aggregate real wages or real profits cannot be increased by inflationary tactics, the real wages of a particular union, or the real profits of one firm or industry, can be increased at the expense of others. More compellingly, if one refrains while others make the utmost use of their immediate market power, that one loses while the others gain; and there is no assurance that his restraint would bring any material reduction in the general threat of inflation. On the business side, firms are not supposed to reduce prices until competitive pressures impel them to do so; and we have seen that in strongly-concentrated industries these pressures act sluggishly, and profits due to inno-

---

[1] The need for such price reductions has been stressed by R. J. Saulnier, Chairman of the President's Council of Economic Advisers, *New York Times*, Aug. 26, 1959.

vation are not diffused until the improvements have become standard practice. As for the consideration that liberal profits expose them to wage demands, a firm is likely to see this logic in reverse: if wage demands are coming in any case, it is well to have the wherewithal to meet them.

(18) In view of all this, it is not surprising that the typical pattern is one in which wages increase more than the industry's productivity, and prices increase in some sort of correspondence with the excess, which represents an increase in wage cost per unit of product. (See table and chart that follow, from exhibits of Theodore A. Anderson, Hearings, Joint Economic Committee, 1959, Part 7, pp. 2156-7.)

TABLE I.—*Percentage changes in prices, wages, profits, productivity for 12 manufacturing industries from the 1st quarter 1955 to 1st quarter 1959*

[Percent]

| Industry | Prices | Wages | Net profits as percent of net worth | | Output | Productivity[1] |
			1st quarter 1955	1st quarter 1959		
Iron and steel..............	+26.5	+34.8	11.2	11.7	+11.6	+11.3
Nonelectrical machinery	23.2	20.6	8.7	7.1	9.6	8.9
Electrical machinery	20.7	19.5	12.0	10.7	5.4	0
Motor vehicles	17.7	17.7	23.6	19.1	—25.1	—1.7
Fabricated metal products ..	13.8	19.5	8.4	5.9	7.1	8.2
Paper and allied products ...	13.0	21.2	10.3	8.5	17.7	14.7
All manufacturing	+10.6	+20.2	11.4	10.0	+12.0	+ 9.3
Tobacco	8.7	23.0	7.3	12.0	18.1	30.2
Petroleum and products	6.7	24.8	12.6	10.1	9.8	17.8
Rubber	5.6	20.0	12.0	10.0	7.6	9.7
Food and kindred products..	4.8	20.8	7.3	7.8	10.2	14.0
Chemicals	2.7	22.2	13.3	13.0	24.8	20.0
Nonferrous metals	1.9	26.4	14.5	8.2	.6	22.9

[1] Refers to total employees.

It will be noted that, while changes in wages show disparities, they are grouped around a pattern which departs only moderately from the average, the greatest departures being in the metals industries. Disparities in wage increases

CHART I

INDUSTRY PRICE INCREASES WERE PROPORTIONATE TO THE EXCESS OF WAGE RATE INCREASES OVER PRODUCTIVITY GAINS

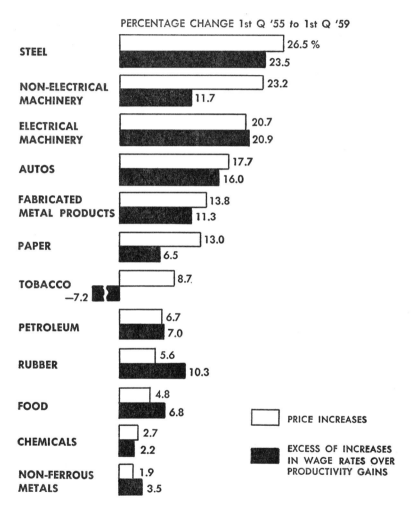

PERCENTAGE CHANGE 1st Q '55 to 1st Q '59

STEEL — 26.5 % / 23.5

NON-ELECTRICAL MACHINERY — 23.2 / 11.7

ELECTRICAL MACHINERY — 20.7 / 20.9

AUTOS — 17.7 / 16.0

FABRICATED METAL PRODUCTS — 13.8 / 11.3

PAPER — 13.0 / 6.5

TOBACCO — 8.7 / −7.2

PETROLEUM — 6.7 / 7.0

RUBBER — 5.6 / 10.3

FOOD — 4.8 / 6.8

CHEMICALS — 2.7 / 2.2

NON-FERROUS METALS — 1.9 / 3.5

☐ PRICE INCREASES

■ EXCESS OF INCREASES IN WAGE RATES OVER PRODUCTIVITY GAINS

are far less than in productivity. In the chart, it will be noted that the sizes of the black rectangles do not represent rates of wage increases but the excess of these over increases in productivity, and they are small mainly where the increase in productivity is large, and where wage increases have in general been above average. These appear to be among the tolerated differentials in the wage structure. Iron and steel once more forms a partial exception, showing slightly more than average rise in productivity, coupled with by far the highest increase in both wages and prices.

As for the above theorems of economic arithmetic, various of them may appear too obvious to need statement; yet it appears also that a full understanding of their purport as a whole is almost non-existent, especially in those quarters where it is most vitally needed. Such understanding is no substitute for a remedy: indeed it may make remedies seem discouraging difficult—as they are—but it is an indispensable first step. In what follows, the picture will be amplified, bringing it closer to the complexities of reality.

3. THE LIMITING ECONOMIC WHEREWITHAL, VARIOUSLY MEASURED

THE increase of physical product, which is the basic limiting economic factor, may be expressed as increase per capita, per worker or per man-hour. The Twentieth Century Fund's notable study found a long-term upward trend per capita of just under 2% per year.[1] The increase per worker is smaller, being about 1.7%, on account of the increase in the percentage of the people gainfully employed. The increase per man-hour would be larger, because of the decreasing trend in hours per worker, and may be reckoned at 2½%, more or less, dependent on the period covered. Output per direct production worker increases faster than output per worker of all sorts. The National Bureau of Economic Research adds a figure per weighted man-hour, weighted to account for the upward drift in the distribution of the labor force between unskilled, semi-skilled and more highly skilled types of workers. Since the weighted man-hours rise relatively to the unweighted, the increase in product per weighted man-hour is less than per unweighted man-hour. These differences in

---

[1] J. Frederic Dewhurst and Associates, *America's Needs and Resources: A New Survey*, The Twentieth Century Fund, 1955.

measurement account for substantial differences in the rates of increase as reported by different methods.[1] The rate of increase has been higher for the period since 1919 than for the preceding period. But from 1953 to early 1959, the real gross national product per capita shows a diminished rate of growth.[2] This flattening out of the trend of growth is something to watch, but covers so short a period that its importance cannot be judged at present.

For our purposes, the important thing is the long-term trend. Productivity fluctuates also with short-term fluctuations in the utilization of industrial capacity; but these are not measures of the sustained capacity of the economy to pay wages and earn profits. The long-term increase in productivity results from technical advances and improved processes, implemented by increased capital per worker and enabling increased output to be turned out with a reduced proportion of direct production workers and an increased proportion of indirect workers, including those engaged in planning and scheduling. Product per unit of capital has increased at times and declined at others—as is natural for the more rapidly-increasing factor—but over the periods 1889-1919 and 1919-1957 as totals, it has apparently increased.[3] This may afford some leeway in the treatment of capital's share of total product.

HOW WAGES AND PROFITS SHARE GAINS

As noted, aggregate wages and profits share the gains of progress in proportions which are stable though not strictly invariable, wages being the larger share, especially in corporate industry, where the most accurate figures are available and where wages have averaged over 70% of gross in-

---

[1] See National Bureau of Economic Research, *Basic Facts on Productivity Change,* Occasional Paper 63; reproduced in Joint Economic Committee, *op. cit.,* Part 2, pp. 295, 301, 309. This paper contains many valuable series, introducing among other things a figure for combined capital-labor input, as a way of distinguishing gains due to technical progress from gains due to increased capital per worker.

[2] See Raymond W. Goldsmith, *op. cit.,* p. 234.

[3] See National Bureau of Economic Research, *op. cit.;* in Hearings, *op. cit.,* pp. 301, 329, 333, 335.

come originating in corporations, and a larger fraction of net income (exclusive of depreciation).[1] Where product per unit of capital has increased, an unchanged share of total product would yield an increased rate of return on investment (before taxes) thus absorbing part of the tax burden. Or labor's fractional share might be slightly increased (as appears to have been happening) without reducing the rate of return on investment. This ability to earn a stable rate of return on greatly increased amounts of capital per worker is presumably dependent on continuing improvements, without which such large increases of capital would reduce, abruptly and drastically, the possibility of securing increased productivity per worker from additions to capital investment. This is the form taken by capital's share in the gains from progress: different from labor's share, but no less important.

As already mentioned, the proposition that total real income is limited to total physical product is subject to qualifications, which become important in wartime. It is, of course, impossible to make a meaningful physical sum out of steel, potatoes, TV broadcasts, etc. Statistically, "physical product" is a dollar sum, deflated by a price index. This works passably well when the conditions as to the spending and investing of income are not drastically disturbed. During World War II they were drastically disturbed when consumer durables became largely unobtainable, and this plus price controls brought about billions of involuntary saving, not matched by peacetime industrial investment. These "savings" counted as "real income," but were not matched by goods and were cut loose from the limits normally set by productivity. As an outcome, by the time price controls and rationing came to an end and normal economic limits were restored, labor had acquired a habit of making gains in "real wages" that were impossible to go on realizing when they had to be validated in goods produced. The importance

---

[1] See exhibits of Edward C. Budd, Joint Economic Committee, *op. cit.*, Part 8, pp. 2523-5, also text, pp. 2520-21. Professor Budd is himself skeptical of the "cost-push" theory of inflation.

of this subjective feature of the war's impact should not be exaggerated; it is mentioned chiefly because it is generally neglected.

The whole war experience was an effective way to set the stage for a postwar period of inflationary wage demands, appearing in the guise of an attempt to regain the wartime condition with respect to feasible gains in real wages. Actually, the economic limits on real incomes remain in force: real wages have kept pace with the increase of real product per worker: nothing has happened to enable them to exceed this limit by more than trifling amounts. Increased money incomes—wages or profits—have no power to break through this limit.

4. NON-INFLATIONARY PRICE-WAGE BEHAVIOR REDEFINED

WE have seen prices and wages behaving in inflationary fashion, and have seen ample reasons for considering such behavior natural. The non-inflationary standard which we have formulated requires that prices should follow economic costs and that increases in wages should be proportionate to increases in economy-wide average productivity, with a trifling leeway for tolerated gains at the expense of profits. But if this is construed to mean that every wage-rate should increase at no more than the economy-wide average productivity, thus freezing existing differentials, at once valid objections arise. This presupposes that the existing wage-structure is in equilibrium, and it never is. Some wage-rates are inequitably low compared to others, and for these, defensive grounds exist for increases in excess of the average. What may be called aggressive excesses are caused by differences in union power, in employers' competitive or oligopolistic position, in rate of increase in productivity and in need to offer premiums to increase supply where growth is rapid. The last is often exaggerated, but does exist. Most of these also occasion differentials in employers' rates of earnings. Where the average rate has been exceeded, movement in the direction of equity or equilibrium calls either for reductions (usually not feasible) or less-than-average rates of increase until disadvantaged groups have caught up sufficiently to bring the differentials within the bounds which the market will tolerate.

Since these bounds are uncertain, the definition of a non-inflationary wage-price structure remains inexact. If a national authority were empowered to give effect to it, the nation-wide average standard could be taken only as an ideal guide, subject to departures for cause, presumably with a hope that downward departures would offset upward ones sufficiently for approximate price-level stability. Stability might be regarded as approximated if those prices marked by various degrees of two-way flexibility are sufficient to mask any upward bias in the rest of the price structure, so that the index as a whole does not have a clearly-predictable trend.

Beyond this begins the real problem of creeping inflation, in which rational policy requires us to appraise the evils and mitigations of the existing condition, and to weigh them against the difficulties, uncertainties and possible ill effects of the available assortment of remedies.

Chapter IV. The Search for Feasible and Effective Remedies

1. ADAPTING REMEDIES TO THE CHARACTER OF THE PROBLEM

U SEFUL discussion of remedies for inflation starts with the rather obvious proposition that we should concern ourselves with remedies that are suited to the kind and degree of inflation at which this study is directed. We should consider what kinds of results the remedies are capable of bringing about in this setting — including possible undesired by-products.

The kind of inflation we are examining is the kind we face at the present time. This means the kind that can be induced by price and wage policies; impliedly when they are the forces that distinctively shape the result: that is, when the situation is not dominated by massive excess demand. If our earlier analysis is correct, this rules out runaway inflation and confines our problem to creeping inflation, or at most to what we have called an "accelerated creep."

The forecasts of the experts appear to embody a near-consensus in anticipating an upward trend of the price level of about $1\frac{1}{2}\%$ per year for the coming decade. This may prove optimistic, and we should be prepared for the possibility of a more rapid upward tendency, and be ready with methods suited to deal with either possibility; but it serves to indicate the extent of the problem as now envisaged by those best qualified to judge.

Another proposition which should be obvious, but apparently is not fully so, is that a proposal does not deserve the name of a "remedy" if it merely designates a desired result, without including at least some general indications of methods by which it might be brought about. Examples would be proposals limited to "increasing output" or "increasing productivity." These offer problems, rather than remedies.

2. "REMEDIES" WHICH ARE PROBLEMS: INCREASING OUTPUT OR PRODUCTIVITY

PROPOSALS to alleviate inflation by increasing productivity stem from the sound idea that one source of inflationary pressure consists of wage increases that exceed increases in productivity; and that this "inflationary gap" may be reduced or closed either by moderating wage increases or by stimulating increases in productivity, or both. But we have seen that the long-term economy-wide increase in productivity is a massive aggregate, which does not change its pace easily: also that since 1953 it has slowed down, after increasing somewhat more rapidly since 1919.

The incentive to improvements increasing productivity is inherent in private enterprise, and is probably intensified by wage increases which increase unit costs of production and challenge the employer to find ways of offsetting the increase by increased productivity. This involves, as an outstanding method, labor-saving mechanization. As to this, the policies of organized labor are a mixture, including official approval by the AFL-CIO of increased productivity as a means to increased wages, plus demands for responsible treatment of displaced workers, while the rules established in actual bargains include some productivity-limiting provisions, which employers would be glad to see relaxed.

In the recent steel settlement, the treatment of this issue appears to have roused more hard feeling on the union's part than any other, and it has been reserved for subsequent adjustment. This may serve to indicate that a major addition to the increase in productivity is not a gadget that can be turned on by pushing a button.

DIFFICULTIES INVOLVED IN IMPROVING PRODUCTIVITY

If the long-term rate should be doubled in, let us say, five or ten years, there is a real possibility that the continuing outburst of productiveness would exceed the rate at which the economy could make the adjustments needed to enable the results to find a market, including modifying existing products and bringing new ones into being, with all the exploratory work that this involves.

For that purpose more is needed than a mere increase of incomes and an explosion of conventional salesmanship to induce people to spend them. An overzealous drive to multiply quantitative productivity, with the emphasis on mechanization and "automation" that would inevitably characterize it, might result in sacrificing important elements of discriminating regard for quality of products. Alternatively, due solicitude for quality might mean slower quantitative progress.

As for proposals to increase output, unaccompanied by technical improvements increasing productivity, this appears to be one way of designating a program of increased production and employment by increasing demand; and the most obvious method would consist of expansionary fiscal and credit policies. In other words, it would be the opposite of the policy of fiscal and credit restriction which is now being followed as an antidote to inflation.

It is difficult to see how both these policies can be, in general and without qualification, consistently anti-inflationary. What is credible is that there is some sort of balance between them at which inflationary pressure *from the demand side* would be absent, while unemployment was kept within reasonable bounds. What these bounds are may always be controversial; and there seems to be no guarantee that such a balance would eliminate inflationary pressures from the side of wage and price policy. These problems are central to the use of fiscal and credit policy as a remedy for inflation.

3. FISCAL AND CREDIT POLICY

WE have already seen that fiscal and credit policies are necessary tools of economic control, and are mainstays in dealing with inflation arising from excess demand; but that they do not reach the causes of pushed-up inflation, and that there is a problem how far they should be relied on to deal with its effects.

These instruments can be used both to stimulate and to restrain, but the two are not simple opposites in their effects, as we have seen in connection with one-way flexibility of prices and the resulting "rachet-action" in response to fluctuations. While expansion of credit may take effect on both volume and prices, the effect of contraction is more likely to be confined to volume, without reducing prices to offset the increase induced by the preceding expansion. Credit controls can be used with general application, as by raising interest rates, or selectively; and selectivity can mean selecting some forms of credit for special restrictions (for example, consumer credit) or selecting some for specially liberal treatment (as by setting up special agencies for farmers or small businesses).

As to the need for using them in the current type of situation, it is urged that, whether the originating impulse to inflation comes from the side of costs and prices or of demand, it brings with it a demand for increased monetary means to finance it, and that a restriction on this increase is the most available means of restraining it.

As against this it is urged that, in view of the downward inflexibility of "administered" prices and wages, credit restriction is more likely to restrict production and employment than money wages and prices. It is urged further that restriction hits the small competitor harder than the huge firm which is more nearly independent of borrowed funds as a source of capital, and that high interest rates are an element in increased costs.

On behalf of restriction it has further been strongly urged by W. W. Riefler that an expected inflationary trend of whatever origin generates a superstructure of hedging transactions which involve increased demand, making credit restriction appropriate for combatting them. It appears that, in connection with the tax laws which allow deduction of interest as a cost, it may be profitable to borrow, even at very high rates of interest, to invest in appreciating assets.

[50]

This argument is open to the objection that in that case high interest rates would check normal productive expansion before checking the superstructure of more speculative hedging transactions at which, on this theory, they are primarily aimed. This appears to point to a need for selective rather than general restrictions, if they are to be used in such a situation; and this would raise a fresh array of problems, not only as to the basis for selection, but as to the means of maintaining it against all the available means of circumvention, whereby credit used literally for one purpose may set capital free to be used for a different purpose.

"REALISTIC" EMPLOYMENT STANDARDS

It is often urged, in connection with credit restriction, that we must adopt "realistic" standards of employment. The purpose of this self-evident phrase depends on the policy-intent that is read into it. There is some level of output, short of a job for every qualified person, at which localized shortages and surpluses both exist, and the market, not being theoretically "perfect," and giving weight to the burdens of occupational and regional shifts, does not bring them all together.

It is possible that the surpluses may exceed the shortages but that the shortages may outweigh them in their effect on the level of prices, leading to upward pressures. Thus a standard of employment might be set, above which a balance of inflationary pressures of the demand sort would be felt, but which would be lower than Sir William Beveridge's famous definition of full employment, and lower than many persons would find satisfactory. If this is all that is meant by a realistic standard, it is open to little objection.

The crux comes if inflationary pressures of the pushed-up sort appear when employment is clearly below this standard. Then the "realistic" standard might be taken to mean a reduction of output and employment until the inflationary pressures disappear. The trouble with this, if the present study is correct as to the behavior of the wage-price structure, is that this point would not be reached short of a really drastic depression, such as we are not prepared to bring upon ourselves by deliberate restrictive policy.

ADEQUACY OF FISCAL AND CREDIT POLICIES

At this point the supposedly realistic employment standard becomes thoroughly unrealistic. Restrictive fiscal and credit policies will not be intentionally pushed this far, and it seems clear that they should not be.

The tendency to undue reliance on such policies stems partly from default of other readily-available remedies, and is fortified to the extent that the belief prevails that the real cause of inflation is always excess demand, to the exclusion of any independent role of price and wage policies. An added factor in this line of thinking is the view that it is wrong to "accept" even the smallest degree of inflationary trend. This view is commendable if it means that we should remain dissatisfied and should continue to seek further remedies consistent with our general scale of economic values. It becomes dangerous if it is construed to mean that we must insist on a quick stamping-out of all traces of inflationary trend, using for the purpose the most readily-available methods: namely, fiscal and credit restrictions. The danger is that this would mean harmful restriction of production and employment, without eliminating the inflationary trend that derives from price and wage policies. The latter policy would mean that we should be so unwilling to accept anything short of perfection in the elimination of inflationary trends that we would accept instead something seriously imperfect in the matter of production and employment.

This discriminatory scale of values appears just as unsound as the opposite kind of discrimination, which makes ultra-full employment a paramount value to be pursued regardless of inflationary effects. The indicated conclusion is that fiscal and credit restrictions are useful and necessary in dealing with inflationary pressures where excess demand is involved, but that it is a serious mistake to place upon these policies the burden of complete elimination of inflation.

4. INCREASING THE FORCE OF COMPETITION

COMPETITION is the most natural force tending to reduce prices or keep them from rising; and our model of non-inflationary behavior for prices was patterned after the specifications of a free and flexible competitive market, in which prices closely follow the levels dictated by costs. And it is precisely because actual pricing processes follow this model so imperfectly that they exhibit the inflationary tendencies we have been analysing. Thus the most natural and logical remedy for these tendencies is to make the economy more competitive, chiefly by strengthening the antitrust laws and their enforcement.

The desirability of the end in view is hardly open to question. As to the prospect of attaining it by this route, there are grounds for hoping for improvement, but hardly for a quick and revolutionary breakthrough. Antitrust policy has been moving ahead ponderously for seventy years; and skeptical observers entertain doubts whether it has kept pace with the opposing forces, which center largely but not exclusively in increased size and concentration.

Even where a new legislative enactment or a new judicial interpretation has important potentialities, it takes time and repeated litigation to feel them out; and the result may be a process of mutual adaptation in which business adjusts itself to the new doctrine while resisting proposed extensions that threaten practices regarded as legitimate, and the boundaries of the doctrine in application are worked out with an eye to permitting practices that are judged genuinely essential to healthy business operation.

EXTENSION OF ANTI-TRUST POLICY

The main traditional line of policy consists in combatting understandings and agreements. Here substantial further results appear to depend on extending the concept of collusion to the kind implied in "conscious parallelism," within limits set by the need to spare the kinds of parallelism that are inherent in normal competitive meeting of rivals' prices. In practice, this seems to mean forbidding it only so far as it is implemented by common practices which make it more complete than independent competitive action would bring about.

For example, the digesting of the results of the anti-basing-point rulings of 1948 — the biggest single step in this area — appears to be still going on, without prospect of producing a general rule against competitive freight-absorption.

Fragmentation of existing oligopolistic giants, if it merely substituted a Big Five or Big Six for a Big Three, might somewhat increase competitive pressures, but would not basically alter the factors that lead to full-cost pricing and downward inflexibility. More drastic fragmentation, even if backed by new legislation, would face enormous practical difficulties, with uncertain results. Big firms would presumably still be able to pass cost increases on to their customers; and might be under pressure to do so, to avoid eliminating weaker competitors. For this last, a fundamental remedy would require changes that would reduce the differences between firms in costs and other features of competitive strength; and such changes would be necessarily slow. Feasible moves on this general front should be encouraged, but they do not promise an early and complete cure for the condition we are considering.

COMPETITIVE STANDARDS FOR UNIONS

The same appears at least equally true of proposals for enforcing competitive standards on unions or reducing their monopolistic powers and practices. Subjection of unions to the antitrust laws has been proposed, without clarifying what it would mean in a market where bargaining is already in the hands of national and international unions. Enforced fragmentation of existing unions appears unthinkable on political grounds, and would raise a mass of problems, starting with the scope of units that would be permitted, and the means of preventing concerted action. Feasible action includes some whittling away of coercive tactics that extend beyond the original intent of the Wagner Act and of later legislation establishing the right of collective bargaining.

Some attempt might be made to define the conditions under which an employer would be protected in filling strikers' places; but the recognition of strikers' tenure of their jobs, in the absence of special grounds to the contrary, is too firmly established to be dislodged from the code of approved practice.

Areas of possible action include limitations on the extension of the boycott, including secondary boycotts, and the more hotly controversial issue of protecting the freedom of a worker to work without joining a union in an establishment in which a recognized union exists. In these areas little is likely to be done in a Presidential year, and in the meantime study may be recommended. It should properly be guided by a presumption against general and inelastic rules, and in favor of preserving a range of freedom for experimental adjustment and for adapting practices to differing conditions, including differing attitudes of unions and of employers. Useful forms of action are possible, but none of them promise to make the setting of wages a competitive act.

INTERNAL AFFAIRS OF UNIONS

On a somewhat different basis are proposals for internal reform of union abuses, including standards of custodial responsibility for funds, protection of individual members' rights against arbitrary or tyrannical action by union officials as well as by employers, more democratic procedures and standards of integrity that would prevent the betrayal of the members' interests by "sweetheart contracts."

Whatever may be said for the last two, it is probable that they would tend to increase, rather than diminish, the kind of cost-raising pressure in the wage bargain that can lead to increased prices. John Dunlop has said: "Indeed, it is likely that we shall have to pay for internal labor reform in the form of some further wage increases as officers are made more timid or insecure and their powers to deal with dissidents are limited."[1]

---

[1] See *Wages, Prices, Profits and Productivity*, 15th American Assembly, 1959, p. 145.

It has often been suggested that increased security of tenure for union leaders might reduce the kind of competitive pressure to which they are subject, which tends to exaggerate their demands. They are often more understandingly moderate than their members. The problem, of course, is how they may have the kind of security that will free them for statesmanlike policies, without also gaining the kind of power that tends to corrupt.

5. THE BALANCE OF FOREIGN PAYMENTS AND THE GOLD RESERVE

OUR policy with regard to the balance of payments is governed by a number of difficult requirements. Continued foreign aid is needed, and to finance it we need a favorable balance on the rest of our accounts. Such a favorable balance accords with the interests of American firms which encounter foreign competition, either from imports or in their own sales abroad; and their workers share this interest. We are also committed to supporting increased freedom of international trade and exchange, including the objectives of the International Monetary Fund. Our recent heavy outflow of gold has so far served a useful world purpose in the strengthening of foreign currencies, which the war had left weak; and the balance of expert opinion seems to indicate that some small further outflow would be similarly useful, so long as our reserves against the growing mass of foreign dollar credits are not endangered. The exact danger point is uncertain, but unchecked outflow is clearly a potential future threat.

The most useful way of reconciling these requirements is to make our products more competitive internationally by ending our domestic inflation — if we can — thus the importance of this problem is reinforced. The threat can also be reduced if our European partner nations, in their present strengthened economic position, are able and willing to assume a larger share of the burden of aid to underdeveloped countries. A simpler and more dangerous method would be for this country to impose trade restrictions, thus reinforcing our inflationary trend by protecting it against a natural corrective check, inviting retaliation and endangering the vitally necessary effort of the free world to progress toward reduced trade barriers. Such moves on our part should be made only for really compelling reasons and with the utmost caution.

CONSIDERATION OF DOLLAR DEVALUATION

Some are contemplating devaluation of the dollar in terms of gold. This would be a positive inflationary force in this country, in addition to occasioning unforeseeable international reactions and possibly undermining the subjective imponderables that underlie such qualified monetary stability as the world possesses. Such an unsettling measure would be warranted only by an urgent emergency, which the present situation does not present. Devaluation has also been urged as a means to a return to a gold standard, which it is hoped would become worldwide. For this purpose it is urged that the present monetary value of gold stocks is insufficient, relative to the growing volume of world trade. This raises problems too far-reaching to be discussed here, including methods of preventing the purpose in view from being defeated by further inflation. Also, if gold stocks are insufficient because world trade is expanding faster than the gold supply, the question arises whether repeated devaluations would not be called for, tending to demolish what remains of the feeling of gold's stable value.

A more feasible and less risky remedy would be to increase the efficiency of the separate countries' gold and currency reserves by handling them in more integrated fashion. Worth considering as a palliative for this country is a reduction of our reserve requirements against our domestic currency, leaving more gold free to meet foreign claims. But elimination of these requirements — also suggested — might threaten the imponderables already mentioned.

To sum up the whole discussion so far, it has dealt with various kinds of remedial action that might be useful, and the combined effect of which might be substantial. But it has revealed none that offer a confident promise of complete elimination of the kinds of inflationary pressure we are discussing. This being the case, it is natural that thinking should turn to direct public action on the setting of prices or wages or both, with or without compulsory power.

6. DIRECT PUBLIC ACTION ON PRICES AND WAGES

PUBLIC action may range from general to highly selective, and from authoritative fixing of prices and wages to mere fact-finding. Remembering that remedies should be proportionate to the severity of the problem, and that the current dimensions of the problem are very moderate, it is understandable that practically no one proposes the general use of authoritative controls to deal with the present situation.

The experience of World War II left a widespread conviction that the indefinite use of such controls in peace-time would be fatal to the essential character of a private-enterprise economy. It may be worth while to recall that the wartime controls were adopted with the utmost reluctance on the understanding that they were temporary emergency measures; and that it was virtually impossible to maintain them after the end of the war, though they could have been of service in at least the early stages of demobilization.

They were necessary because the wartime excess demand was too great and too one-sided to be successfully neutralized by fiscal and credit measures, while "mobilization by price" would have produced violent and self-defeating distortions. None of these features is present now. What is even more to the present point, the wartime controls demonstrated the capacity to slow a potentially runaway inflation down to an accelerated creep, but not to eliminate the creep, despite resort to a general price-freeze, and later to a "hold-the-line" order.

This experience affords no basis for expecting such controls to stamp out a slow inflationary creep. This is well to

[58]

remember if we are tempted to resort to them for that purpose because less drastic controls have failed to accomplish it. War-type controls would presumably fail also.

LIMITED CONTROLS OF PRICES AND WAGES

Actual proposals for direct controls of prices and wages, to deal with the current type of inflation, generally contemplate limiting the controls to a few industries which are large and important, are highly concentrated, have played a leading role in price-wage spiral movements and are judged to have a "bell-wether" quality. Consideration of such controls might be placed on the agenda of an inquiry focusing on the steel industry, which is a leading candidate on all four grounds, but might raise objection to being singled out. Action on prices might be limited to the power to suspend increases suspected of an important inflationary effect, pending inquiry.

At every point, difficulties would be presented by criteria for selecting industries, type of action and agency.[1] Inquiry might lead to findings of fact only, or to recommendations with or without enforceability. Enforceable orders would need to observe judicial safeguards and procedures which would make action cumbrous, where flexible promptness is of the essence. The need for considering hardships inflicted on poorer competitors might lead to findings too cautious to be effective in preventing a slow creep. Where wartime price orders allowed a range, prices were sometimes raised to the maximum. And if hurdles are placed in the way of raising prices, this may make firms more reluctant to reduce them, where reduced costs would permit.

Advisory recommendations might be less bound by judicial requirements of due process, but are fully dependent on voluntary compliance instead of only partially so, while the pressure reinforcing voluntary compliance is that of public opinion. This depends on active influence by a well-informed

[1] For an excellent analysis of different possibilities of public action, see Emmette S. Redford, Joint Economic Committee, 1959, Study Paper No. 10, 29 pp.

minority, with more general support from larger numbers who have sufficient interest and information to give expression to the most-neglected interest in such cases — that of the consumer — and to weigh it fairly along with other interests.

Whether public opinion could be well enough informed, and well enough balanced, and able to hold a sufficiently-sustained interest in a sufficient number of cases, remains an open question, and a highly important one.

It is sometimes proposed to restrain price increases while leaving wages uncontrolled, hoping that this may influence the course of wages indirectly, by stiffening the resistance of employers to inflationary wage demands. A variant, intended to avoid the difficulties of price control, is J. K. Galbraith's proposal that an employer granting a wage increase should be debarred from raising prices for six months thereafter.

Such a dual-purpose plan might well encounter the combined opposition of employers and a great majority of workers. As to the effect of either kind of plan, one clear probability is that unions would refuse to abate anything of their wage demands, many of which the employers would feel they could not absorb. In that case, the result might be a series of unusually-stubborn strikes.

On that score, the postwar history of the steel industry is not reassuring. If repeated and prolonged strikes are an index, the industry has bargained stiffly; and in the resulting settlements it has led the procession in wage increases, in inflationary excess of wage increases over productivity increases, and in price increases.[1]

As for findings on wages, we have seen why they are bound to allow considerable latitude, even if the inflationary character of the "industry-by-industry" standard were more widely understood than it seems to be at present, and if boards or arbitrators took the economy-wide average increase in productivity as an initial *prima facie* guide to a

---

[1] Cf. Table I and Chart I, pp. 40, 41, above.

non-inflationary wage. It seems that they would encounter so many well-founded grounds for exceptions, most of which could be counted on to be in an upward direction, that they would end with something very like a compromise with the "industry-by-industry" standard, being driven to this by pressures that would prove irresistible.

So far, our search for remedies has revealed numerous ways of putting external restraining pressures on the exercise of the powers and discretions possessed by the parties to bargains on prices and wages in the current type of economy. In the aggregate, these pressures appear capable of having material effect. Moderate degrees of these pressures are already exercised, and it seems likely that they deserve some credit for the moderate extent of the present inflationary trend. But our search has also revealed limitations, sources of resistance and means of evasion, which preclude confidence in an ideal result.

The effectiveness of any remedies depends on an attitude of understanding cooperation. To the factors underlying such an attitude we may next turn.

7. THE BASIS OF A VOLUNTARY SYSTEM: RESPONSIBLE ATTITUDES GUIDED BY UNDERSTANDING OF REQUIREMENTS

In dealing with this problem, it is clear that in our group-organized economy, intelligent action by private bodies in the pursuit of their particularistic interests is not enough. Numerous leaders, from President Eisenhower down, have called for more responsible attitudes toward the public interests involved. What may be less obvious is that this also is not enough, without a clearer and more widespread understanding of what the public interest requires in this connection.

In the latest steel dispute, the union presented demands that would clearly raise costs, the employers held out for their version of a non-inflationary wage adjustment (meaning one that would not raise costs) while reserving their own final judgment as to that part of a non-inflationary standard which is concerned with price and profit policies. In the resulting deadlock, the public interest boiled down to the paramount need to make some kind of compromise that would keep the industry running after the expiration of the eighty-day Taft-Hartley "cooling-off" period. Of the compromise that resulted, the best that can be said on this score is that it is less inflationary than some previous compromises in this industry; but since they were leaders in the inflationary procession, that is small praise.

THE NEED FOR VOLUNTARY RESTRAINT

The need for voluntary restraint presents a problem rather than a solution: a problem as to how effective it can be and how it can best be promoted, back of which lies the problem of the standards of economic conduct which it calls for. It is a fundamental principle of any society based on voluntary action that the amount of freedom that can be retained— freedom from public controls on the one side and from the coercions of private actions on the other—is measured by the extent to which the need for public coercion is lightened by the members' voluntary acceptance of the requirements of living together. In the present case, the "members" include powerful organizations with established quotas of economic discretion and power; and the required restraints are not "obvious and simple," as should be evident from the preceding analysis. Preliminary progress has been made. If it is to become effective, it will require understanding leadership and the development of appropriate representative agencies for formulating standards and disseminating them.

In the absence of these elements, skepticism of its efficacy is widespread, and is amply warranted. The unimplemented approach has been effectively ridiculed by Ben W. Lewis, under the title of "Economics by Admonition."[1] He pictures the demand for responsible action as a call to substitute

---

[1] See his paper of that title in *American Economic Review*, May, 1959, pp. 384-398.

altruism for private interest, and in its vague light to solve an insoluble complex of problems as to what the true interests of society really requires.

This exaggerates the problem and minimizes the available resources for dealing with it. The problem is one of restraint on self-interest, not its displacement in favor of altruism; and the identification of non-inflationary behavior does not present an insoluble complex of problems, but is quite comprehensible, and capable of being much more widely understood than it is.

MOBILIZING THE FORCES OF UNDERSTANDING

Admonition alone will not supply this ingredient. It calls for organizing and mobilizing the forces of economic understanding in such fashion that the results may reach and fertilize policy. This is best promoted by enlisting the active participation of those who make and carry out policy on prices and wages, at the same time that their thinking and their preconceptions are challenged in constructive fashion by people grappling with these problems constructively from the public standpoint. That indicates that representatives of business and labor should be in the process but not in control of it. Otherwise, they would be too unlikely to modify their preconceptions, which in turn are likely to lead to deadlock or to inflationary lines of least resistance. In addition, there is need of widely-informed public opinion, such as can be promoted through active discussion by many sorts of interested groups and agencies, and their work will be made more effective if competent analysis, such as is available, is systematically presented to them.

This affords a problem in organization, for which a wide variety of suggestions have been made, involving different principles of method and strategy. There are parts of the work that can presumably be best done in isolation from such things as a specific labor dispute, but not in such complete isolation that the results are in danger of appearing irrelevant to any particular policy decision. The ultimate end in view is to influence such decisions.

[63]

One of the most delicate functions of liaison in such an organization would be a two-way liaison between the more generalized studies and specific policy decisions, in which each would supply materials to the other, and interchange between them might progress as fast as conditions proved to be ripe for it—which might not be very fast. A general body could hope to issue reports that would be useful in promoting understanding; but it may be optimistic to hope that the time might come when it could usefully follow the example of the British Cohen committee in suggesting limits for wage increases for the coming year. If such suggestions were attempted before the interests concerned were ready to give them some weight, they might be worse than ineffective. The foundations need to be laid by effective and patient clarification of issues. The importance of this work, and of effective organization for it, is great beyond the possibility of overestimate.

PROBLEMS OF ORGANIZATION

Numerous problems of organization arise. Should the body in question be active only at intervals or should it be a standing body? Should it consist of, or be headed by, public officials; in which case should it be a cabinet committee or an enlargement of the work of the President's Council of Economic Advisers or of the Joint Congressional Committee, or independent of all these? Should it have a permanent staff, and if so, how should that staff be related to existing bodies, public and private, from whose investigations it should draw material? To what extent does its orientation differ from those of these existing bodies in ways that would require independent gathering of material?

As to scope of study, one notes that there are studies directed to monetary policy and other studies directed to the impact of price and wage policies, both oriented at the problem of inflation.[1] The result is that neither one can appraise

---

[1] By way of illustration, one might cite the Report of the Fourteenth American Assembly: *United States Monetary Policy;* and of the Fifteenth: *Wages, Prices, Profits and Productivity.* Both deal with the problem of inflation, and exhibit

the effect of its subject-matter on inflation without taking into account the way in which its action is conditioned by the subject-matter of the other. Does the resulting overlapping study represent the best division of labor?

If it is decided that there should be a basically private body, it must be initiated and organized somewhere, as the National Commission on Money and Credit was set up by the Committee for Economic Development, or as the successive meetings of the American Assembly are sponsored by Columbia University. Rarely does an issue command such intense and widespread interest that a completely new organization may be formed around it which will—in these days of organizational inflation—command general and serious attention. In any case, one of the major ends in view is liaison between the backgrounds and viewpoints of public officials and of private individuals and groups, representative of special interests and of varied viewpoints on the community interest.

Arthur F. Burns, former Chairman of the President's Council of Economic Advisers, has proposed that the Advisory Board on Economic Growth and Stability including cabinet officers and Presidential advisers, be converted into a standing body, meeting regularly under the chairmanship of the President, and equipped with staff.[1] In that case, workable relations should presumably be set up with an interdepartmental committee under the chairmanship of the Chairman of the President's Council of Economic Advisers. Dr. Burns also approved the private Commission set up by the Committee for Economic Development. The hearings of the Joint Congressional Committee on the President's Annual Report afford a mine of material deserving systematic utilization by competent groups in addition to the reports of this committee itself. John Dunlop has proposed a three-day conference of leading representatives of labor and manage-

---

[1] See 14th American Assembly, *op. cit.*, pp. 217-18, cf. pp. 88, 113.

---

the salutary overlapping mentioned above. This is an example of the private, occasional body, without continuing organization for dealing with this problem.

ment, convened by the Secretary of Labor, after the Committee's hearings have been made available, which would receive analyses of the economic outlook from the Secretary of the Treasury, the Chairman of the President's Council and other key public officials.[1]

The present writer would be inclined to stress the importance of a body consisting of private personnel in which representatives of special-interest groups would constitute a minority, of a standing character and equipped with staff, which would make available not only arrays of factual material, but professionally competent economic analysis, carried to the point of showing its implications for policy.

From among these and other proposals it should be possible to select appropriate and promising instrumentalities for backing up appeals for responsible conduct with cogent analysis of what kind of adjustments this calls for, so that the combination may stand some chance of influencing actual behavior.

A DIFFICULT BUT NECESSARY TASK

This task is enormously difficult. It needs to embody principles that are simple in their essence, such as the basic arithmetic we have discussed. When it comes to application, it is necessary to give sufficient recognition to the varied conditions that have to be reckoned with, without losing sight of the principles and lapsing into empty platitudes. Suppose this task is reasonably well accomplished, how much can it be expected to accomplish? The answer probably is: not very much in the closely-visible future. In time, it might make mediation or fact-finding more effective in the direction of less inflationary settlements; but only to the extent that it succeeded in modifying attitudes on both sides which appear at present to be firmly held by those in the seats of power. This is a long-term undertaking.

But it is a necessary undertaking if we are dissatisfied with the slow creeping inflation which appears to be the best

---

[1] See 15th American Assembly, *op. cit.*, p. 148.

result we can hope for from the other remedial policies we have discussed, and if we want to go on working for further improvement, without incurring the greater evils of general and direct control of prices and wages, or the really drastic restriction of production and employment that would result from a determined attempt to stamp out inflation by severely restrictive fiscal and credit policies, in the face of the existing downward inflexibilities of prices and wages. The indicated probability is that we shall be living with a slow creeping inflation for some time; unless we are so unwilling to tolerate it that we resort to remedies carrying alternative evils that are worse—and perhaps even then we should not fully attain the desired price-level objective.

8. CONCLUSION

As regards policy toward the effect of price and wage policies on inflation, the implications of the present study point to avoidance of compulsory controls of prices and wages, and avoidance of the more subtle temptation to rely on fiscal and credit restrictions to do more in the way of restricting increases in the price level than they can properly and safely be called on to do. With regard to the special problem of the international exchanges and the drain on this country's gold supply, this appears to want watching; but does not appear to call for either a raising of the dollar price of gold, or a reversal of the policy of promoting freer international trade, in favor of a revival of national protectionism. Within these limitations, this study points toward prudent and circumspect experimentation on a variety of fronts, supplemented by efforts to induce the voluntary adoption of less inflationary bargaining behavior by a combination of investigation, consultation and mutual education, rather than by mere exhortation to more responsible conduct.

Assuming that these methods are used in combination, with reasonable success, the best prospect for the coming decade appears to be a gradual diminution of the inflationary gap between wage rates and productivity, by moderation of wage-rate increases and somewhat more rapid rise in productivity, accompanied by some increase in downward price flexibility, until the overall course of prices, including the flexible ones, becomes mildly fluctuating and uncertain, and the expectation of future inflation dwindles until it ceases to be a substantial aggravating element. If this happens gradually, the abnormal premiums attached to inflation-hedging investments may shrink to a more rational capitalization of expected material growth (as distinct from price-inflation) without disastrous collapse. One hopes that the moderate decline of the stock-market now taking place (January, 1960) may prove to be an adjustment of this salutary sort.

To sum up: so long as the inflationary trend maintains its present slow pace, it is not necessary to eliminate it completely, this year or next, but it is necessary to start working on it more effectively than at present. In the words of Arthur F. Burns: "Fortunately, we still have time as a people—though by no means unlimited time—to arrest the growing belief in the inevitability of inflation and to organize our economic affairs so that faith in the integrity of the dollar may be re-established."[1]

---

[1] See "Monetary Policy and the Threat of Inflation," in *United States Monetary Policy*, Fourteenth American Assembly, p. 213.

DATE DUE

30 505 JOSTEN'S